The Sacred Monstrous

The Sacred Monstrous

*A Reflection on Violence in
Human Communities*

Wendy C. Hamblet

LEXINGTON BOOKS
Lanham • Boulder • New York • Toronto • Oxford

LEXINGTON BOOKS

Published in the United States of America
by Lexington Books
An imprint of The Rowman & Littlefield Publishing Group, Inc.
4501 Forbes Boulevard, Suite 200, Lanham, Maryland 20706

PO Box 317
Oxford
OX2 9RU, UK

British Library Cataloguing in Publication Information Available

Library of Congress Cataloging-in-Publication Data

Hamblet, Wendy C., 1949–
    The sacred monstrous : a reflection on violence in human
communities / Wendy C. Hamblet.
        p. cm.
    Includes bibliographical references and index.
    ISBN 0-7391-0615-5 (cloth : alk. paper) — ISBN 0-7391-0743-7
(pbk. : alk. paper)
    1. Violence—Moral and ethical aspects. I. Title.
BJ1459.5.H36 2003
303.6'01—dc22   2003020506

Printed in the United States of America
♾™ The paper used in this publication meets the minimum requirements of American
National Standard for Information Sciences—Permanence of Paper for Printed Library
Materials, ANSI/NISO Z39.48–1992.

for my father,
whose generosity toward the suffering
was so pure that it went unnoticed.

for my mother,
who noticed.

Contents

Preface

apologia

Most human beings, whatever their particular affiliations and loyalties, seem to exhibit a genuine concern for the ethical viability of their actions. Most people seem dedicated to benevolent—or at the very least justly reciprocal—relations with other human beings. However, it is equally clear that violence plays an enormous role in human affairs. The terrain of human encounter is, and always has been, a bloody field of engagement. Perhaps Dostoevsky expresses this most succinctly through the voice of Ivan Karamazov when he has Ivan observe that the earth is soaked from its crust to its center with the tears of a suffering humanity.[1] Evidently today, as throughout the long history of the human species on earth, an immense abyss divides the humane intentions of the individual from the brute realities of human interaction around the globe.

Much energy has been spent, and worthily, in the attempt to unriddle the mystery of human suffering. This has, in fact, been claimed as the prime impetus of philosophy, and has often been cited as the force that drives the social and technological sciences. However, though suffering is rarely encountered far from the field of violence (in one or another of its myriad forms), though it is clearly the force that carves out human history, though it is the connecting thread that links all wars and revolutions, all acts of torture and terror, all tyranny and genocide, violence is rarely singled out as worthy of philosophical analysis. Despite the stunning banality of violence, virtually no philosophical attention has been given to the possibility of suffering as a byproduct, and violence as a constitutive element, of human engagement *as such*.

It is no simple oversight that this topic has escaped philosophical address. In an important article "Penser les Massacres," Belgian political scientist Jacques Semelin discusses three aspects of the problem of extreme violences (*crime de masse*) that cause researchers to shrink from its analysis.

> The first is psychological in nature: avoiding a research topic that triggers horror and repulsion is understandable. The second is moral: faced with acts of pure savagery, how is it possible to prove 'scientific neutrality'? The compas-

sion felt for the victims leads spontaneously to the condemnation of their tor-
turers. The third obstacle is more specifically of an intellectual nature: the phenomenon of massacre defies understanding. It appears to have no 'sense,' nor
to 'serve' any purpose. We tend to write it off as man's 'folly.' [2]

Semelin's "third obstacle," the understanding of human evil as mere "folly," the
work of fools and madmen, describes pithily the conviction of the mass of ob-
servers of the human drama, whatever their various perspectives and disciplines,
scholar and non-scholar alike. Most of us seem convinced that violence only
occurs when a breakdown in normal relations occurs, under anomalous conditions that erode people's humaneness or under the ideological sway of "monsters" like Hitler, Mussolini, or Stalin. Despite the striking everydayness of violence, few seem willing to see it as a constitutive element of human engagement.

So the subject of violence has rarely been taken up for serious research and
when it has been addressed at all, it has rarely been a philosopher who has addressed it. We find brilliant scholarship by political scientists and historians as-
sessing particular instances of violence in the world, yet few attempts at serious
philosophical analysis of violence in itself, and never an analysis of violence as
an elemental feature indigenous to human community. None, but a very few
anthropologists in the intellectual line descending from Konrad Lorenz, have
approached the problem of violence as anything but anomalous, as a malfunc-
tion or collapse in the norm of healthy human engagement.

In this work, I intend to address this philosophical gap. Since histories har-
bor the secrets of human ways of being, I shall take up the claims of prominent
anthropologists regarding the normalcy and "naturalness" of violence for human
beings. That is, I shall unfold the philosophical implications of the anthropological claim that violence is an essential, not an incidental or anomalous, feature of
human community. I hope to draw compelling connections between the ways in
which, according to the anthropologists, the earliest human communities were
formed in the dawn of human time and the ways in which we continue today to
"engage humanly"—the ways in which we continue to carve out our identities as
individuals and as human groups over against alien others. I shall propose that
there may persist dispositions toward destructive behaviors, deeply embedded in
the human psyche, functioning as mechanisms of identity-construction, and in
the symbols and binding logic that order our cultural institutions and systems
and dictate the prescriptions and prohibitions that delineate codes of proprietous
conduct. I shall suggest that these dispositions toward violence provide a compelling explanation for the paradox of human history—the overwhelming destructiveness that configures the terrain of human engagement on earth, despite
the noble ideals and aspirations meant to guide that engagement.

The issue of the truth or falsity of the anthropologists' theories is not what
is at stake here. Though I am certain that causal connections do exist in the
world of experience, I leave the infinite mystery of their connectedness to those
far wiser than myself. I am interested solely in what is to be gained ethically—
what might inform the quest for what Socrates calls, in the *Republic*, "the right

conduct of life"—when human beings entertain the possibility that their ways of being-together, and the systems and institutions that shape and record the historical fields of their engagement, are fundamentally and integrally murderous. What is to be gained when humans understand violence as constitutive of human engagement itself?

Grounded upon anthropological theory, this work necessarily attributes great import to histories—individual, communal and specific. Thus, and ironically, this philosophical treatment of violent histories will rest on the further assumption that the most powerful aspects of human identity are not to be located in the history of ideas that we call philosophy. Nor can they be found in the chronology of political events or the catalogue of human achievements that we call human history. Rather, this work will suggest that the deepest secrets of human identity may be buried within a history of performances that comprise our "ritual histories." I shall propose that the powers that configure thought and incline action in the modern world may be traced back to an experiential history, a long-forgotten register of archaic practices—rituals of expulsion and torture and murder. These histories may continue to exercise a powerful effect upon present modes of being-in-the-world because their forces may be *in* us as inclination and disposition. They may hold us through our very identities, through the ways we understand self and world, through the loyalties that bind and connect us, through the mores and manners of our cultures, through the very "civilizing processes" that we believe constitutive of the forces of good in the human world.

The reader will note certain tensions and ambiguities that arise in this work. These tensions and ambiguities stem from a fundamental paradox that underlies the project, the paradox of attempting to articulate the problem of violence in a language always already infected by violence, itself a product and vehicle of the histories of violence that hold us in their ideological sway. This makes for a performative contradiction that constantly threatens to unseat the work. It raises the problem: how to articulate clearly and distinctly an ethical argument that militates against clear and distinct moral judgments. How do I convey violence *as a problem*, as an undesirable phenomenon that demands our focused attention, without myself falling back upon the logic of polar oppositions that, by attaching to phenomena exaggeratedly clear and distinct moral meanings, manifest and re-enact the very mechanisms I will claim elemental to human destructiveness?

In its very attempt to have ethical impact upon its reader—that is, in comprising an "ethical" work—this philosophical exercise cannot help but replicate the moralizing gesture that enacts "demonization." It cannot avoid a moralizing rejection of certain behaviors and, by inference, of certain people who practice those behaviors. This work must make moral judgments. It must distinguish between good homes and bad homes, healthy modes of dwelling and unhealthy, and, ultimately, if only by implication, between worthy human beings and the not-so-worthy. It must, therefore, in accomplishing its ethical task, ultimately find itself guilty of the very violation that it is seeking to cure. It cannot help but repeat the "counter-cultural rejection" that it will, ultimately, condemn as endemic to, and constitutive of, the violence that characterizes human engagement. In attempting to trace out the ambiguities that inhere in the problem of violence, this work will prove to be itself performative of those ambiguities, just as it will prove to be itself performative of the violences that configure the terrain of human engagement.

Another violence of this work inheres in the assumptions from which its analyses of homes arise. In identifying the task of "home-craft" as always, on some level, violently structured, I have deliberately inclined my characterization of identity-formation toward aggressive self-assertion, discounting from the start any possibility of benign human engagement. That is, I have resisted any distinction between the concepts of violence and force and, in so doing, I have left little room to account for what might be argued the "truest" acts of self-definition, acts of selfless sacrifice for the benefit of helpless others. This failure is a rank falsification of the lived experience of human goodness. A great many instances of purely benign acts are recorded, for example, in the testimonials of Holocaust survivors.

I have chosen to overlook these instances of pure human goodness and to begin from the rather hyperbolic assumption that all human engagement is, at least to some degree, violent, not to deny the many heroes and heroines that have been eulogized for their selfless acts of kindness, but to provide a more ethically charged backdrop against which to stage a radical critique of current trends in identity work. I want to frame an arena of thought that emphasizes the growing aggressiveness manifest in the arrogant self-righteousness of superpowers and in the bloodlust of struggling ethnic groups.

This admittedly falsified framing gestures toward the peculiar nature of the ethical work that this essay seeks to accomplish: it seeks not to offer a truth but to tell a "likely story" ("noble lie"?) about the secrets of "human nature." By characterizing dispositions toward alien others as fundamentally murderous, I hope to open a meditation that counters modern tendencies toward aggressive self-assertion and blind self-righteousness. Perhaps such a meditation might help to cultivate a predisposition to examine oneself critically even where one's intentions are felt to be most benign. I hope that the proclivity to understand as potentially violent one's own ways of being might exercise a limiting power over the violent inclinations peculiar to human beings, inclinations witnessed in the everyday brutalities that hit the news, in the endless catalogue of atrocities recorded in our history books, and in the theories of the social scientists that I rally here. I trust that facing the possibility of one's own deep-seated propensity for violence may hold the thinking person to more exacting ideals of self-evaluation, and to more taxing standards of compassion, generosity and welcome than might otherwise be called forth in the inviolable purity of the "sacred homespace."

However, because I have begun from the assumptions that violence inheres in all human encounter and that blind egoisms comprise the fundamental structure of the vital function of identity-construction, the work remains, by logical necessity, unable to distinguish between the structural possibility of violence and the empirical necessity of violence. I am aware, and concerned, that ultimately this failure may collapse altogether the viability of ethical endeavor. The claim that all encounter is essentially violent can, ultimately, be deployed to justify acts of violence as necessary and *in any case* unavoidable. And it can be used to excuse and thus extend our already overwhelming capacity for apathetic non-response to victims of atrocities. Furthermore, I am concerned that the inevitability of ethical failure implied in the claim that all human encounters are, on some level, violational recommends guilt, despair and a sense of victimization as appropriate psychic responses to the problem of violence in human communities. Since these are themselves major progenitors of destructive behaviors, I am wary that my plea to minimize violence may elicit the opposite of the desired effect.

Thus, I mean this *apologia* to communicate the double sense of the term— defense and confession. I admit to being part of the problem of violence, even in my speculations addressed toward minimizing our violent ways. This study of the problem of violence in human communities does violence. It does violence to the concept of violence in speaking of the problem of violence in human communities as though it were a single phenomenon, stemming from a single source or, at least, from common sources. It does violence to the reality of human goodness in permitting violence no benign forms. This work does violence, naïve and dangerous violence, to the complex realities of human communities, large and small, each infinitely unique.

Furthermore, in this work's having a project, in its comprising an "ethical" work, in its assumption that identity work can be tracked, analyzed, described as such, and monitored *from within*, this study speaks, necessarily, from the tyrannical (if false) position of the autonomous Western subject, about the tyrannical (if false) integrity and coherence of human communities. In so doing, this work cannot help but reassert as though unproblematic the reality of these subjective inventions. But, most importantly, this study does violence because it speaks, at times with a dangerous passion, about phenomena that demand moralizing responses. The great risk of this work is that it too will manifest the immense abyss that divides benevolent intention from brute reality in the world. My "swan song," meant to soothe the savage urges, may very well achieve the opposite consequence. It may well awaken the beast.

I can only say, in defense of this endeavour, that I have approached my task most timorously, that I have made a conscious effort to minimize the violences in this discourse on violence. I have tried to avoid generalizations and overly simplistic moral observations, though I found this an enormous challenge given my acute personal awareness of the suffering that accompanies violence about the globe. I also found it a great challenge because these features are encrypted in our languages and seem to insinuate themselves into even our most self-critical moments of thinking. I have attempted to combat the tendencies toward generalization and moralization by setting more complex local examples of identity formation over against the more hyperbolic grand structures, to trouble the neat simplicity of the latter.

I have taken up, only obliquely, the complicated question of the link between gender and power relations. In an effort to avoid insensitivity to the statistical realities of domestic abuse, I have self-consciously employed masculine terms in reference to the abuser, concomitantly slipping into feminine terms when speaking of the victim. However, I have attempted to complicate that gendered reading of the problem of violence and to move it always toward the priority of the victim, whatever the gender, by gesturing toward the complexities of power and the diverse tools of tyranny employed across the human landscape by men, women and children. I have also tried to address justly the infinite complexity of the interconnectedness of victimization and aggressive self-assertion. That is to say, I have attempted to combat, if not dislodge, the "logic of domination" and the mechanisms of "counter-cultural rejection" that I will claim to fire violent responses, by demonstrating that each human being is *both* victim and abuser. Moralizing responses become logically untenable, if not impossible, once one accepts this single fact.

As I have said, I make no truth claims about the work that follows here. I mean it simply as a "swan song" to raise questions about the way we human beings assert ourselves in the world over against alien others. Most of all, I mean to disturb the self-satisfied complacency of those of us in well-fed Western capitalist democracies who find it easy to forget the faces of the hungry children, as *invisibly* present *here*, sheltering under bridges and in doorways in our own fair lands, as *there*, in the famine-struck deserts and the strife-torn ghettoes on the far side of the globe.

Notes

1. Fyodor Dostoevsky. *The Brothers Karamazov*. tr. Constance Garnet. New York: Barnes and Noble Books, 1995. Book V.4. (paraphrase).
2. Jacques Semelin. R.I.P.C., Vol.7, no 3. 08/02/01. 1. Jacques Semelin is a Research Fellow for CADIS/ CNRS (associated with CERI, Paris).

Chapter 1

Ritual and Mythical Beginnings

Much attention has been given, in contemporary philosophy, to the power of mythical figurations in structuring our living worlds. There is little doubt, since Plato's *Republic*, that the stories we ingest, particularly as children, have remarkable influence in shaping the kinds of human beings we will become, the forms of action to which, under given stimuli, we will be prone, and the metaphysical/ideological framework that will figure the horizons of our lifeworlds. Myths are entirely pervasive of the human world, even in the modern era that, understanding itself to be *post mortem dei*, also considers itself myth-free. The ideological presence of myth pervades not only our narratives, but our understandings of self and world, structuring notions of right and wrong (good and evil), dictating the social codes that prescribe appropriate behaviors and prohibit the inappropriate, and underpinning every human artifact that comprises our political, social and economic systems.

The power of myth to shape the being of a people has long been acknowledged by the social scientific community and can hardly be overrated. René Girard writes: "There is no term in any language that is not accompanied by mythological inflections."[1] Alasdair MacIntyre warns that our stories are "intellectual prophecies" that become over time "social performance."[2] MacIntyre believes that a people's moral thinking and the actions they take up as "good" are structured largely by their narrative histories. Mircea Eliade has also written convincingly of the power of myth to shape a culture. He asserts that the foremost function of myth is to provide exemplary models for all significant human activities. Even in cultures where myths have "died" and people believe themselves freed from their mythological heritages, mythological ontologies and their ideological messages live on in the assumptions underlying cultural practices. The mythical "exemplars," it turns out, are most accomplished at re-clothing

1

themselves in fresh symbolic garb that can parade in the austere light of the new secular day. Thus the experts conclude that myths form the very core of our psyches and are the stuff of which we, as individuals and as members of human communities, are made. Myths tell us who we are, from what we have come and who we are meant to be *as human beings*.

Myths, as stories served up to our children in the nursery, as vehicles for religious truth, or as the narrative matter studied by scholars of antiquity, mask their immense and serious power behind a playful pretense of falsity. Consistent with the word's origin in the ancient Greek term *mythos*, myth signifies in advance a deviation from the verifiable. Its telling *as myth* disclaims any responsibility to truth. Ancient tales were almost always prefaced with disclaimers like: *ouk emós ho mythos* (the tale is not mine). Perhaps the muses speak through the tale-teller. Perhaps a god has lifted the poet up to view mundane matters from loftier climes. Whatever the superhuman source, the wisdom of the tale is admittedly beyond human reckoning—and question—so there is no necessity, or indeed point, in challenging its authenticity. Even the know-nothing Socrates admits to "knowing" about love, since the priestess Diotima has given him a myth.[3]

Myth, *qua* legend, is not bound by any fixed form. The same tale can show up in song, as an epic poem, in tragic theater, as a moral allegory in a Platonic dialog or as a digression in Pindar. Nor is it bound to any fixed content. Myths are polyvalent; that is, they have many voices and say different things to different ears. So there are many tones and accents to the truths communicated through myth. Yet, despite the breadth of myth's forms and the variation in its content, even a casual perusal of myth, from however wide the cultural sources, will strike the reader with an appreciation of the frequency of certain themes.

Common to almost all mythological tales of origin is the positing of an original golden age where human beings shared a primordial home in harmony with the god(s), a home where human beings lived happy and peaceful, free from toil or sorrow, guarded and nourished by their divine progenitors. The second most common feature of myths of origin is the theme of the "fall" of humankind from this primordial bliss. Humans show themselves to be too corrupt to live up to divine expectations, so they are cast out of the heavens, abandoned to the earth, to wander and struggle for their survival. Another pervasive theme describes a primal ritual whereby order (*kosmos*) is wrought in the universe. *Ab origine*, order is imposed by a wondrous act of might upon a threatening measurelessness (*kaos*) by unambiguously "good" powers. Thereafter, whenever unrest threatens the cosmos anew, at the timely changing of the divine guard or when human beings prove so troublesome as to require divine discipline, a radical act of violence brings renewed political and social order to an unruly universe.

Myth's starkly polar imagery makes its moral and ontological messages clear, even to a child. Humans are unworthy; they are guilty and corrupt. Even our divine creators have abandoned us. Life on earth is a death sentence in an alien setting, not a loving nurturance at the breast of the earth mother. And life on earth can be chaotic. When it is, only radical acts of violence from an authority transcendent to the local law can set the situation right again. Yes, myth's messages are clear. Dangerously clear.

However, the elusive, dreamlike quality of myth, its advance disclaimer of responsibility to the truth, persuades us to let down our guard when listening to these stories. We can enjoy the charming tales they tell precisely because they are overtly fantastic. Therein resides the paradox of myth. Myth is as much our "intellectual history" as the history we record in history books and teach our children in schools. Myth bears the surface seal of *pseudos* (lie, deceit) but communicates, nevertheless, the notion that that seal is impressed upon an underlying substance of truth. There is a sense of the solemn about these tales, as there is about all things time-honoured. Perhaps that sense resides in the claims of superhuman origins or perhaps in their grander view of things, their sacred vista over the landscape of time and truth. Whatever the reason, we *feel* the seriousness of the tale, even knowing it to be fantastic. We *sense* its sacred character beneath the façade of illusion.

A single telling grants the impression of truthful substance beneath the cosmetic falsity. Over time, the telling and retelling of myths gains narrative histories, however fantastic, a certain "reality." Anthropologists explain that myths reify in the language and symbols of a culture and substantiate in their political, social and economic systems. Myths take hold of the intellectual life of a people by shaping the "conceptual universe" that they share. That is, mythological symbols and the connections that marshal those symbols (ontological and logical) form the symbolic storehouse of a culture from which a people's vision of reality is constructed. The possibilities for understanding self and world are configured within the horizons of this "conceptual universe."[4]

With the turning of the epoch, people will come to see their old tales as false.[5] They will label them "myths," perhaps retire them to the nursery as mere amusement for children, and thereafter cease to consider their content risky— because falsity admitted can be plainly viewed *as such*. However, the symbols that underlie the mythical images, their ontological assumptions, and the logic that connects the symbols and communicates their peculiar ideological messages can remain doggedly active and functional. Because of their uncanny power of persistence, it was believed for some time, after Mircea Eliade, that myth was the "origin" of ontology and ideology, prior to other forms of historical persuasion. What the experts on myth failed to see, in that early era of speculation, was that the power they had traced *through* myth into the conceptual universe of a people did not originate with mythical narrative. The real culprit, prior to myth itself, was occluded from the scientist's view.

However, it is now generally accepted that a power far greater than that of myth resides in the "rituals" that precede the legends, those seemingly meaningless, endlessly repeated performances of series of actions, practiced over millennia by all human and animal cultural groups. Experts had long believed myth prior to ritual since new rituals do develop to dramatize the truths of myths and to recapture that powerful forces believed resident therein. However, scholars now agree that ritual is not merely a secondary manifestation of some prior spiritual belief, as Eliade had contended. Rather, the ideas and values expressed in myths are conceptualizations and articulations of earlier *performative truths* communicated first *through bodies* in the medium of ritual. Ritual is prior to myth and not the other way around. That Neanderthal man already had an elaborate ritual life is evidenced by deposits of bear skulls, the use of red ochre and paint, and the uncanny collections and treatment of human bones and skulls at grave sites. These testify to complex systems of ritual practices long before humans developed the physiological equipment necessary to articulate speech.[6]

The term "ritual" boasts an extensive and rich history. The term derives from the ancient Greek word *dromena* that signifies a breadth of acts accomplished: things done, things said, things shown forth. The term was generally utilized in reference to the cult mysteries whose "showings" and "doings" were not only mysterious, having to do with calling forth and participating in ancient secrets, but were also known to be dangerous, bloody and murderous, overseen by the "dark gods." The term "ritual" is used in everyday parlance as well as in ethological scholarship to speak about patterns of stereotyped demonstrative behaviors that are obsessively regulated to the most minute detail. That is, rituals are forms of non-verbal communication that "speak" through patterns of actions. These actions can be perceived, identified, charted, described, and repeated, in consequence of an underlying, organizing "logic" re-conveyed with each successive repetition. Walter Burkert explains:

> Interaction in any society may be both pragmatic and communicative [but] we speak of ritual if the communicative function is dominant.[7]

Rituals communicated ontological and ideological messages through active performance long before they came to linguistic expression in the elusive symbolism of myth or achieved conceptual clarity in religious ontologies and formal ideologies.

Rituals, because they are performatively communicated, are far more powerful than myth. They come to be far more deeply carved into a people's being because they are etched, with each repetition, into the flesh of each participant, into the memories silently harboured in bodies, and finally into social and political institutions, codes of conduct and patterns of dominance and exchange. And, because rituals are ostensibly meaningless even to the participant, they are far more difficult to rationally confront than their conceptualized reformulations in myth. Their effects are thus far more insidious and far more difficult to root out. This is why we may assume that rituals both predate and outlast their mythological expressions, comprising the real and lasting force behind the flowing and fleeting images. They *pre*configure, across the lineage of their evolving expressions in myth, the powerful undercurrents that give rise to (ostensibly) "new" ideas, "new" energies, and "new" exemplars to guide human behavior.

Modernity is a constantly changing locus of belonging. Old loyalties soon lose their luster and charm when considered in the light of the "achievement ethic" that, in the capitalist world today, governs much of our thought and behavior. As mediocrity consumes diversity under the leveling effects of democracy, as democratic ideals of autonomy and freedom drive wedges of suspicion between fellows, as the traditionally rich network of family relations is worn thin to an obsessive nuclearization that impoverishes notions of responsibility, as a frenzied consumerism devours other value systems and replaces them with an insulating competitivism, the individual feels more and more her isolation, her estrangement, her powerlessness—the fragility of the human.

Nevertheless, heavy investment in the system limits the ways in which these frustrations can be voiced, and limits the ways in which differences can be legitimately located, asserted and expressed. Thus frustrations can more easily find outlet projected upon those outside the system or upon foreign systems *as such*. Therefore, it is reasonable to assume that modern forces (urbanization, industrialization, and democratization) have given rise not to a myth-free, ritual-free secular world, but rather these forces serve to substantiate the ontological and ideological messages communicated in ritual and myth, reaffirming their bifurcated vision of reality, their exaggeratedly clear view of moral realities, their obsessions with purity and contamination, the "demonization" of differences that compels moralizing responses, and their compulsive conviction of the "innocence" and inviolability of the homespace.

Centuries and even millennia after the supposed death of ritual practices, long after the discarding of the factual content of myths, the mechanisms that call forth violent responses may still endure, shaping the ways that people engage. The old destructive ways of being may live on as bearings in people's attitudes and undercurrents in their behavior. These bearings and undercurrents may lie entirely dormant, it is true, throughout the whole life of an individual. No claim to the contrary could ever be categorically substantiated. On the other hand, these undercurrents and bearings may seethe and fester beneath the thin veneer of modern complacency, ready to flare to the surface when feelings of powerlessness and despair burst through the apathetic shell that contains them.

We have seen again and again in the modern era that, where feelings as powerlessness, victimization and despair are at work, an individual or a people may attempt with dangerous zeal to establish a familiar territory—a homespace—from which site to establish and assert self-definition and forge allegiances with familiar others as emblems of entitlement to continuance in an overcrowded world. In the trajectory of violent histories, mythical truths and ritual ideologies and their "ordering" paradigms may silently take charge. Where people feel helpless and threatened, detached and morally confused, home-craft may take on a distinctive structure. It may become an obsessive project that regulates or suppresses differences in the interest of stable and integrated identity. It may seek to purify its "sacred" domain by rejecting alien "contaminants."

Notes

1. René Girard. *Violence and the Sacred.* tr. Patrick Gregory. New York: Crossroads Publishing, 1996. 154.

2. Alasdair MacIntyre. *After Virtue.* Notre Dame, Ind.: University of Notre Dame Press, 1984. 85.

3. Plato. *Symposium.* 199 ff.

4. See Walter Burkert. "The Problem of Ritual Killing" in *Violent Origins.* ed. Robert G. Hamerton-Kelly. Stanford, California: Stanford University Press, 1987. 147-176. 152.

5. John S. Dunne. *The City of the Gods: A Study in Myth and Mortality.* Notre Dame, Indiana: Notre Dame Press, 1978. See opening pages of Introduction.

6. W. Burkert. "The Problem of Ritual Killing" in *Violent Origins.* 147-176. 152.

7. W. Burkert. "The Problem of Ritual Killing." 150.

Chapter 2

Ritual In-*form*-ations

the anthropologists' theories

In the beginning was violence.
(E. Levinas. "The Temptation of Temptation"[1])

Men are always saved after the death of the deliverer.
Men reject their prophets and slay them,
But they love their martyrs
And honour those whom they have slain.
(F. Dostoevsky. *The Brothers Karamazov*[2])

The Problem of Histories

The ontological assumptions and logical mechanisms that structure our actions and are played out in our experiences issue from an existential ground far deeper and more complex than can be fathomed by rational analysis, and they exercise a power far greater than that of rational argument—a fact that, until the post-modern era, perhaps Nietzsche alone fully appreciated. Nevertheless, persistent mechanisms structuring sequences of actions can be rationally analyzed. They can be identified, tracked and employed as an interpretive device to indicate possibilities for future actions. Persistent mechanisms have been traced over lifetimes, over generations of lifetimes, over centuries and even millennia.

This is because sequences of actions repeated over long periods of time become inscribed into the bodies of the participants, just as, over time, sequences of practices become inscribed into the "bodies" of participating cultures—into

7

the painful recollections of their elders, into the submissive timidity of their womenfolk, into the fleshy expectations of their young. Bodily practices come to settle deep into the resentment-riddled, guilt-prone, swaggering or timorous materiality of their progeny. Actions repeated over long periods become "ritual-ized." That is, they take on, by virtue of their time-defying persistence, a porten-tous seriousness—a "sacred" import—in the minds of practitioners and their inheritors. This is how traditions are formed and come to assume a "timeless validity." The practices that mark individuals as belonging to a cultural group, and that mark cultures as self-identical over time and distinct from alien others, come eventually to be obsessively regulated with strict governance over the place, time, and circumstances of their repetition. All manner of valuable—and not so valuable—practices become part of a people in this way. People become wedded to their customs ("rituals" in ethological parlance). Giving up *what we do* comes to be equated with giving up *who we are*, forsaking the glory of our pasts and betraying our destinies.

Thus rituals acquire a time-honoured weight in a community. Their com-municative power extends the identity and indeed often, in the beginning, the very life of the group across vastly fluctuating politico-economic circumstances. Rituals comprise a medium of continuance, a powerfully conservative force, precisely because they compose a kind of communication, the most concrete kind. Rituals, as sequences of actions rooted in pragmatic interactions, convey the traditional "wisdom" that regulates the life of the group—matters of hygiene, sexual practice, marriage custom, rites surrounding birth and death, and espe-cially rites of passage initiating newcomers to full membership in the fold.

Many of the practices persisting in this way were originally adaptive and many remain crucial to the healthy continuance of the group. Whether they re-main adaptive within the evolving social unit or not, their "goodness" is cate-gorically affirmed with each repetition by each new generation, perceived as empirically tested and reconfirmed across time. Ritual traditions thus become emotionally-significant, utterly tangible, materially embedded realities, and though their origins and functions may have become utterly lost to the group's memory or shrouded in myth, their communicative power remains fully func-tional even without memory or understanding.[3]

Therefore ritual traditions do not simply convey rationally-identifiable and meaningful informations—ideologies. In fact some rituals do not convey any explicit messages at all, but, rather, they comprise an in-*form*-ing process that directly "affects" (in all the multivocal senses in which this term is classically understood) the addressee as much as the addressor. Many scholars, like Mircea Eliade, have argued that the truths expressed in myths comprise ontological and ideological disclosures that dictate visions of cosmic reality and patterns of dominance and exchange. However, if myths are the symbolic expression of deeper, older, *experiential* truths, as contemporary scholarship now agrees, then it is reasonable to accept the claim of many anthropologists that our thinking and our behaviors today remain in-*form*-ed by the practices repeated by our distant forbears.

Experiences speak to the core of our psyches. They seep into the very sinews of our bodies and carve themselves into our feelings and desires so that new "needs" crop up where old practices have gone before, new needs that now *require* satisfaction. Walter Burkert explains this biological process called "imprinting":

> Biology has drawn attention to the phenomenon of "imprinting," an irreversible modification by experience, distinct from normal learning by trial and error; it is most notable in early stages of life. In fact, religious attitudes seem to be largely shaped by childhood experience and can hardly be changed by arguments; this points to the imprinting effects of ritual tradition.[4]

There are other indications that ritual practices have powerful and lasting effects. Since the rituals practiced by early human communities were almost entirely rituals of murder, torture and expulsion, long-standing rituals may very well have manipulated the evolutionary chain. After all, ritual murders, ritual castrations, and ritual expulsions are very real extinction, very real closure of certain genetic lines, very real ejection from the genetic pool of the social group. Thus, the powerful individuals who oversaw the ritual life of the community (priests, kings, medicine men) could not only self-select for survival. They were in a position to fix and manipulate the biological—as well as the religious and moral—composition of the group and define, by elimination of the "contaminating" elements, the markers of identity peculiar to it.[5]

For a number of sound reasons, then, the power of ritual histories and their mythological expressions needs to be taken seriously. Thus it seems important for thinking human beings to examine not only their present rituals and their recent histories, for traces of the in-*form*-ing violences, but to consider as well the rituals that were practiced by our ancestors in the distant past of human time. Granted, this examination of self and species may expose things more comfortably left concealed. As Edward Shils has asserted in his article "The Sanctity of Life":

> To persons who are not murderers, concentration camp administrators or dreamers of sadistic fantasies, the inviolability of human life seems to be so self-evident that it might appear pointless to inquire into it. To inquire into it is embarrassing as well because, once raised, the question seems to commit us to beliefs that we do not wish to espouse and to confront us with contradictions which seem to deny what is self-evident.[6]

Thus I do not expect that an exposure of the continuity between our current supposedly benign self-defining practices and the bloody practices whereby human communities have historically taken shape will prove reassuring of our assumptions of the moral progress of the species. But, hopefully, this exposure will require us to look at ourselves differently. Perhaps it will unsettle the self-righteous assumptions peculiar to Western capitalist nations and force us, as individuals, to question our own behaviors and suspect a personal quota of the legacy of violence.

Ancient rituals have proven fascinating to experts from a wide range of disciplinary fields. Psychologists, behaviorists, classicists, philologists, literary theorists, historians, zoologists and anthropologists have contributed to the rich discourse on this intriguing subject. What strikes me as uncanny is the number of correspondences among the various theories, correspondences all the more significant for the diversity of inductive bases grounding the various disciplines, for the dissimilar approaches and methods of investigation, and for the diversity of assumptions and impulses driving their pursuits for insight. I shall assume that the mysterious correspondences among the theories can offer us a firm ground for thought about the nature of our species' early ritual histories.

The Exaggerated and the Grotesque

The debate over ritual's penetration into human psyches and cultural forms first began in the 1960s with the shocking claim of behavioral physiologist Konrad Lorenz that human adaptive rituals, designed to ensure species survival, had turned maladaptive early in the dawn of human time, thwarting the healthy development of the species in the direction of a grossly exaggerated aggressiveness. In his masterpiece, *On Aggression*,[7] Lorenz does not simply claim that humans maintain beastly instincts, but, rather, that the beasts are more adaptively evolved than humankind and thus less disposed than humans to murder their own kind.

Lorenz explains that, in early humans, the development of cultural artifacts rapidly outpaced biological evolution. Humans developed an arsenal of weaponry of unparalleled destructive potential and variety of form, while failing to develop the inhibitors, natural to animals, that would discourage their turning those weapons upon each other. Lorenz's point is precisely that humans are different from animals (a point lost to many of Lorenz's more critical readers[8]). Animals adapted more effectively to environmental changes along a slower evolutionary path so that healthy braking mechanisms kept pace with their destructive potential. Human beings were not so "evolutionarily" lucky.

Intra-specific aggression is originally an adaptive process, Lorenz explains. It develops in species to serve four important selective functions. First, it helps to maintain an even distribution of animals over a given inhabitable area. Second, it aids in sexual selection. The rival fight naturally selects the hardier, more aggressive fighters to command both territorially and sexually. Thereby a third benefit is accomplished. Family defense is enhanced since the selective process favors the evolution of particularly strong and courageous defenders of family and herd. Fourth, intra-specific aggression leads to the establishment of a ranking order in the group, a feature Lorenz notes as crucial to the development of advanced social life in higher vertebrates. Ironically, the "pecking order" that results from aggressive rivalry ultimately brings stability to the community since it creates a social situation in which fights between the members are limited to the service of sorting and ordering functions.[9]

Intra-specific aggression, then, serves important functions in the healthy evolution of the animal group and remains adaptive where its limits are intact. Under restricted conditions, it accomplishes the cooperation and cohesion that bind the group and enhance its chances for survival in hostile environments and over against other animal groups. Humans, however, are distinguished from animals in this regard: humans evolved very quickly into the kinds of beings who were not restricted by their environment. They gained a relative freedom from environmental exigencies very early in their evolution, beginning with their mastery of fire. This remains the crux of the problem for humankind's exaggeratedly aggressive urges. In a particularly disturbing passage, Lorenz tells:

> Obviously, instinctive behavior mechanisms failed to cope with the new circumstances which culture unavoidably produced even at its very dawn. There is evidence that the first inventors of pebble tools, the African Australopithecines, promptly used their new weapon to kill not only game but fellow members of their species as well. Peking Man, the Prometheus who learned to preserve fire, used it to roast his brothers; beside the regular use of fire lie the mutilated and roasted bones of *sinanthropos pekinensis* himself.[10]

Lorenz explains that when intra-specific aggression exerts selective pressures uninfluenced by environmental pressures, it can develop in a direction that is markedly maladaptive. Evolution of the species can then take a turn that can be irrelevant or detrimental, or even catastrophic to the survival of the species.

> Aggressive behavior can, more than any other qualities and functions, become exaggerated to the point of the grotesque and the inexpedient.[11]

Humans have been particularly exposed to the ill consequences of maladaptive selective processes, according to Lorenz. The "grotesque and inexpedient" destructive intensity of the human being is a "hereditary evil" that drove the earliest men to slaughter their fathers and brothers and neighbours. Lorenz asserts that selective processes gone astray are what we are still witnessing today in elaborate displays of aggressive prowess, those perverted elaborations of swaggering machismo and overblown bravado still practiced in obsessively patriarchal societies.

In nature, fighting is an ever present phenomenon and the weapons and behavior mechanisms that serve that process are highly developed. Yet fights between intra-specific rivals rarely end in death. Encounters between prey and predator may result in death but this does not constitute aggression, on Lorenz's terms. According to Lorenz, a victim sought for food does not incite "aggressive" impulses any more than a chicken in the refrigerator incites human aggression. Animals stalking food do not display the "expressive movements" that signal aggression. On the other hand, those signals are clearly displayed in the

way young boys thrash each other in the schoolyard or young men brawl in bar-
rooms, or even in the heated explosions characteristic of political debates or
sports contests (among both participants and spectators). I venture the speculation that the mere invention of atom bombs by beings as flammable as we are
testifies to the perversion of human aggressive impulses toward "the grotesque
and the inexpedient."

Lorenz distinguishes between rituals transmitted by tradition and those
passed by heredity, but the distinction is a moot one. Rituals that have begun as
traditional practice, like the redirected aggression ritual (a ritual that prevents
aggression toward the mate or another intimate member of the social group by
diverting it toward a more remote or defenseless object) become, after long
practice, part of what Lorenz calls "the fixed instinct inventory"[12] of the species.
This indicates that rituals take hold one way or another. They will eventually
become identifying marks of the group whether consciously accepted, enforced
and transmitted to the young, or absorbed into the bodies of the participants to
develop into needs that become, in turn, driving forces that require their means
of discharge.

Perhaps the most stunning among Lorenz's many shocking claims is the
priority of aggression rituals to rituals of love, nurturance and friendship. The
latter, explains Lorenz, developed over many generations as transformations of
"ceremonies of appeasement," rituals meant to redirect aggression by placating
the attacker. Intra-specific aggression—selective practices grown "grotesque and
inexpedient"—are *fundamental* to the human world, thousands of years older
than love or friendship, and source and origin of the latter. Lorenz asserts:

> intra-specific aggression can certainly exist without its counterpart, love, but
> conversely there is no love without aggression.[13]

Even laughter in its original form was probably an appeasement or greeting
ceremony developed from redirected aggression.[14] I suggest that we can still
witness its aggressive roots in the cruel way that children (and many adults)
ridicule others who are mentally or physically different or culturally alien to the
home group.

Lorenz's project is to demonstrate that, by observing the natural behavior
patterns of the animal world, we will discover not only much that will remind us
of our own behavior, but much that warns us that our behavior may not be under
the strict governance of reason that we believe it to be. Lorenz is committed to
collapsing the popular fallacy (the fallacy upon which was originally founded
the discipline of anthropology) that all that is "natural" is adaptive. Our inclinations may all too often follow blindly the patterned materiality of our histories
and, since our histories are primarily murderous, that is a problem for healthy
human engagement. Many people today still refuse the evolutionary explanation
for the development of humankind on earth. It not only contradicts their religious myths and challenges the notion of human centrality in the cosmic drama,
but the claim that we are evolved from apes offends their sense of species supe-

riority. However, if Lorenz is correct, the common origin of human and beast is not at all the problem. It is the *differences* between us and the animals *since* the forking in the evolutionary chain that causes our greatest problems.

Lorenz has fallen from the foreground of the discussion of human nature largely because he employs the language of "instincts" to speak about human behavioral dispositions. The concept of instinct has lost favour in philosophical and social scientific discourse not merely because that term reminds us of the discomfiting fact of our animal ancestry, but because the admission of instinctive behaviors suggests a "biological fatalism" that precludes the viability of analytical solutions to human problems.[15] Instincts are morally blind and thus it is disturbing to think our behaviors under their sway. But it is important to note that Lorenz himself was no biological fatalist. He firmly believed that we can, over time, alter even fundamental dispositions. But his final analysis of the human situation was not overly optimistic, as the concluding words of his book testify:

> how abjectly stupid and undesirable the historical mass behavior of humanity actually is.[16]

Lorenz does not intend to clear human beings of the charge of maladaptive behaviors. Rather, he wants the history of that maladaptativeness to stand as an ethical warning to the species. Unless we develop healthier rituals of engagement, we are doomed to the biologically just deserts of species extinction.

The "two-containers" Ideology

Anthropologists attempting to explain human behaviors have not all heeded nor even agreed with Lorenz's warning. However, no future explanatory account of human hyper-aggressiveness could begin without first addressing Lorenz's claims. The evolutionary debates of the 1960s, emphasizing the instinctive nature of aggression, met with the conceptual revolution of the 1970s that shifted the terms of the debate from the instinctive to the sociobiological, emphasizing the ruthless, self-interested competitiveness of the social group over the individual. Both approaches tended toward oversimplification of the problem of human aggression. Both failed to adequately mark the effects of the infinite complexity introduced into the sphere of the competitive by the fundamental survival necessity for cooperation and cohesive group life. Despite these critical failures, later anthropologists of violence remain in general accord with Lorenz's theory and have sought to develop and nuance that originary work to bring it to conceptual fruition. One such thinker is Walter Burkert whose corpus has proven impressive. *Homo Necans, Structure and History in Greek Mythology, Greek Tragedy and Sacrificial Ritual, The Creation of the Sacred, Ancient Mystery Cults* and *Greek Religion* are some of his better known works. Burkert, a classical philologist and anthropologist of religion and culture, approaches the problem of violence in human communities by combining historical and philological research with biological anthropology. The results have been remarkable. Burkert originally assigned to the classical tradition profound importance for the intellectual and cultural development of the West. However, his investigations into classical rituals led him to the amazing discovery that this tradition was itself permeated with symbols and practices from much earlier epochs and different cultural traditions. Burkert came to see that, even in the highest period of classical culture, rituals that were pre-Greek in origin, and perhaps even prehistoric, continued to exercise an unshakable hold over the Greeks, long after the cultural or religious "meanings" of those rituals had been lost, if they ever had been explicit.

The sacrifice ritual is one such pervasive anomaly that continued to accompany festivals, seats of oracles, athletic games, cult gatherings and other mystery ceremonies, theater festivities, state ceremonies and funeral services, long after that ritual had any meaningful resonance with those events or with the religious beliefs of the participants of those events. Burkert's inquiry into the uncanny endurance of these rituals led him to an amazing insight: rituals function in such a fashion that they do not require either belief or understanding to remain operative and effective. Rituals remain onto*logic*ally and ideo*logic*ally functional, even fully disconnected from their *logoi* (stories, meanings, arguments).

This is probably due to the fact that ritual comprises the preverbal medium of religious communication, more primitive and ancient than speech, and therefore logically (and ideologically) prior to stories, myths and religious or philosophical arguments. Rituals, explains Burkert, transmit through imitation "messages" in terms of function.[17] To discover what kinds of functional messages are being communicated through early rituals, Burkert looks to the distant past of the species to the rich palette of ritual life in early hominoids, rituals that centered about life's most significant functions—hunting warfare and mating (including practices involving the search for food, dispositions for fear or flight, aggressive display and sexual customs). Since he is convinced that many of these early rituals have been bequeathed to modern humans across millennia of evolution, Burkert posits a "common mental world" whose symbolic content, functional logic and tone of seriousness have been transmitted to modernity through an uninterrupted chain of tradition.[18]

All tradition consists of condensed, systematized information. The function peculiar to ritual traditions, contends Burkert, is to keep finite the conceptual system of the participating community. Ritual traditions employ, to this purpose, strategies of negation and class-inclusion and exclusion. These strategies, conveyed to and through bodies, constitute patterns and analogies of reality that achieve a "reduction of complexity" that provides a simplified system of cultural "meanings" to orient those who would otherwise feel vulnerable and powerless *vis à vis* the infinite complexity of their environment.

One very effective way rituals achieve this "reduction of complexity," Burkert explains, is through the positing of dual "containers" (good-bad, right-wrong, us-them, pure-impure, sacred-profane, friend-enemy) into which new experiences or phenomena can be easily sorted. From these sortings, then, hierarchies can be constructed and links of causality forged so that reality is reduced to simple and general concepts that bring sense and meaning to the individual life. A radically over-simplified, polarized worldview is the result.

A simplified, polarized worldview functions most effectively as an orienting system. If an "ultimate signifier" (god, chief, king, father) is added to this equation, the system then offers easy solutions to even the most thorny of human dilemmas, resolving, as matters best left to infinite wisdom, those conflicting factors of life that refuse to fit neatly into the two "containers." Even the most oppressive domination, the most insecure conditions, the most unjust distribution of goods can be brought into moral equilibrium by the positing of a transcendent overseer to whom all must ultimately concede, and a transcendent gift system that balances the cosmic ledger in a final accounting.

It is through ritual's "ordering" processes that a culture's "collective representations" are conveyed and communicated to the young of each successive generation as the time-honoured "traditions" of their culture. Through rituals, a "common mental world" of clear and distinct meanings and identifications can be shared by the cultural group. Rituals comprise "the very epitome of cultural learning," states Burkert.[19] It is not merely *that* they are self-reinforcing through the power of resonance, but it is *how* they are made to resonate in the bodies of participants that figures their abiding force. Ritual learning, historically, took place in the context of the harshest forms of intimidation. According to behaviorists, learning is most indelible where memories are painful, humiliating or anxiety-ridden.[20] Ancient ritual practices centered about animal and even human sacrifices, painful purgatorials and excruciating physical mutilations. Bloody murders were often witnessed firsthand. Participants were made to handle, drench themselves and sometimes even drink the sacrificial blood. Whippings, beatings, tortures and murders were administered by them and to them. Terror and pain are certain to leave indelible scars.

Furthermore, rituals were effective conveyors of traditional cultural "truth" because, as educators know, the most effective and instructive events are those that require full bodily participation and activate the full range of emotional responses. The festivities with which each ritual event culminated combined song, dance and laughter, with their repetitive rhythms and sounds, to give vent to the pent-up psychic energies aroused by the tortures and slayings. The festival closures to ritual events, then, completed the full sweep of emotional and bodily participation to make the communal ritual the fullest and greatest of collective experiences. These experiences etched into each successive generation the inviolability of their traditions, concurrently marking the culture self-identical across the flux of time and connecting it with the changeless eternality of the ancestors and the gods.

Burkert demonstrates that the appeal to tradition supplies the rationale for many of a society's practices and institutions. However, since tradition cannot provide the explanatory key to the abiding primacy of the function of ritual itself, Burkert makes this his quest. Finding it a highly significant "cultural coincident" that much of Greek sacrificial practice (care and manipulation of bones of the deceased, for example) matches with reconstructions of Paleolithic hunting culture, Burkert develops a theory of the ritualization of the hunt that provides a primal model to explain the origin of the simplistic, polarized logic that he identifies at the foundation of a culture's "common mental world."

The Paleolithic hunt is one of the earliest communal events and since it was likely, in its original form, highly emotionally-charged, being utterly crucial and fundamental to the needs of the social group, it was probably critical, contends Burkert, to the creative construction of an orienting worldview for the group. Since the hunt was essential to the formation and survival of the first structured societies, the worldview spawned by hunt ritual was likely so functionally efficacious that it has been able to continue in full force over centuries and even millennia, despite radical upheavals in cultural formations along the path of "civilization."[21]

Burkert explains the persistence of the ontologies and ideologies communicated through hunt rituals. During this early stage of human culture, when the only weapons were wooden clubs and spears, hardened over fire, the intense collective energies (mostly anxiety and terror) that were focused on the large carnivores would have heightened the significance of the hunt far beyond the mere gathering of food. The full range of survival strategies would have had to be rallied, paradigms of behavior practiced within the group would have had to be fully restructured, and patterns of ranking and ordering aligned and enforced. These behavior codes ("rituals" in ethological parlance) would have effected a sublimation and rechanneling of the old intra-specific aggressions (identified by Lorenz) into political hierarchies and patterns of allegiances designed to ensure the success of the hunt.

The first rituals probably comprised simple pre-hunt ceremonies that called forth the power of the ancestors and lured the animal into the territory. Then elements were added that funneled and brought to expression the full range of anxieties and energies evoked by the hunt: the hesitation before the event and the shock and guilt at the spilling of the blood of such a significant "other." Later, rituals added disclaimers of responsibility for the murder and "apologies" after the event. Rituals were called upon to establish the fiction that the victim gives himself willingly to the community, participating and cooperating in his own murder. In this way, the hunt could be successfully inverted into festivity and the ambiguous energies of the participants could be purged. Culminating festivities came, thus, to celebrate the beneficence of the self-sacrificial animal while the concomitant distribution of meats occasioned the primal "moment of exchange" upon which political and economic institutions came to be founded.

In Burkert's account, then, the intra-specific aggression that so troubled Lorenz finds a new target in being projected onto the prey, and human beings, now deeply anxious over killing, develop rituals precisely to manage the psychic tensions. A simple original pre-hunt ritual event eventually propagates into more and more elaborate forms until it culminates in the formation of every manner of social code—prohibitions and prescriptions delineating appropriate behaviors in all contexts of social interaction. But perhaps the most interesting and significant feature of Burkert's theory (for my purposes) lies in his claim that the Paleolithic hunt ritual created and reconveyed original ontologies and functional ideologies that continued over vast stretches of changing times to orient the cultural group.

For Burkert, the ritual of the hunt, focusing such intense energies upon a single object-prey, was profoundly creatively productive and thus a complex symbolism gathered about the object and charged it with a dynamic imagery that was layered with multivocal significances. The animal, while remaining animal, became anthropomorphized and divinized, assuming contrasting images that were paradoxical, yet dialectically entwined: male/female, wild predator/friend, evil/beneficent, life-prolonging/death-giving. In time, these polar symbols grew into the full cosmic hierarchy that comprised the "common mental world" of the group.

The conceptual universe thus formed from ritual's creative confusions then evolved and mushroomed into the entire range of mythic articulations. Thus was the lifeworld of the social group created such that

> [t]wo sign systems, ritual and language, came to reinforce each other, to form the mental structures that determine the categories and the rules of life.[22]

Burkert understands the rituals surrounding the Paleolithic hunt to have been so fundamentally stabilizing that they would have come to be repeated outside of the hunt at any time that social order was seen to be in need of rejuvenation or re-solidification. Burkert traces the hunt ritual into many later distinct ceremonial forms, including the myth of the hero, Greek dramatic theater in general and the tradition of the royal hunt. Bloody murder, ironically, articulates the very founding moment of human "civilization." Like Lorenz, Burkert leaves us with a warning. He is convinced that the bloody origin of human community is still evident and its psychological residue threatens to topple the edifice of human achievement. Burkert identifies the cracks in that edifice in the exaggerated seriousness and obsessive rigidity that characterize our responses to the human situation. Echoing Lorenz, Burkert asks: "What kind of a fitness is it that renders people unfit for change?"[23]

Sacred Violence and Identity Crisis

One cannot approach the problem of violence without acknowledging the important work on this subject by René Girard, literary theorist and anthropologist of religion and culture. Girard has devoted much of his scholarly energy and expertise to unriddling the enigma of the connection between violent behaviors and notions of the sacred. In an imposing corpus (*Deceit, Desire and the Novel, La Route antique des Hommes Pervers, Things Hidden Since the Foundation of the*

World, and especially *Violence and the Sacred*), Girard presents one of the most important—if controversial—contributions to our understanding of ritual violence.

Girard's most renowned work, *Violence and the Sacred*, opens with the stunning assertion that violence is endemic to human society. Violence is the catalyst crucial of human community. Religion, explains Girard, arises in response to the need to create an illusion to mask this discomfiting truth. Religion's task is to rationalize the violence by creatively transforming human murderousness into a manifestation of the sacred in the temporal world. Violence takes on myriad forms but these, according to Girard's theory, polarize into two: the "good" violence of ritual (which, by definition, involves excessive regulation) and the "bad" violence that is its evil twin (because uncontrolled), best exemplified in the wars and pollutions that can maintain for generations between feuding families, tribes or nations where there is no ritual outlet for the vengeance. Human beings are able to come together and form communities only through reliance upon the "good" violence of ritual practices, primarily the sacrifice ritual. Girard states: "Sacrifice is the most crucial and fundamental of the rites; it is also the most commonplace…"[24]

Girard is so impressed with the pervasiveness of the sacrificial ritual that he makes the bold, and in my opinion analytically fatal, leap of faith that leads him to claim sacrifice as the *sole* unifying mechanism of the whole of human culture. He asserts:

> There is a unity that underlies not only all mythologies and rituals but the whole of human culture, and this unity of unities depends on a single mechanism, continually functioning because perpetually misunderstood—the mechanism that assumes the community's spontaneous and unanimous outburst of opposition to the surrogate victim.[25]

For Girard, the murder of a sacrificial victim by a unanimous community underlies all social and individual creation—all the structures of human community, all the artifacts of the human world. Language, codes of etiquette, kinship systems, cultural prohibitions, marriage and procreation prescriptions, all patterns of exchange and power, all customs regulating birth and death—in short, all civil, political and social traditions and all artistic endeavor—emanate from this single ritualized origin.

Girard posits an original "dark event," the collective ritual killing of a random victim. All subsequent ritual comprises obsessive re-enactments of the original event in order to assert and reconfirm the "justness" of that original killing, to keep hidden its true randomness.[26] By why the original event? Girard claims that communal murder is necessary to stable community as a consequence of the pervasiveness of a psychic mechanism that he calls "mimetic desire."[27] This mechanism drives one person to value another's object of desire, not as a function of the absolute or subjective value of the object (as is generally supposed), but because the possessor of that object is himself valued and emulated. In this claim, Girard universalizes the Freudian theory of familial rivalry that asserts: I desire my mother only because my father, whom I value, desires her. The problem arises as one approaches more closely to the object of desire. The closer one gets, the more he arouses the animosity and rejection of the one he truly values, the model. Thus arises the paradox of the veneration and rejection that Girard terms the "double bind." In this paradoxical relation, the model remains exemplar and object of veneration but at the same time becomes the enemy—a "monstrous double" of the emulated model.

In Girard's theory, mimetic rivalry is both the motivator and frustrator of human community. Echoing Lorenz, Girard reminds us that human beings lack "braking mechanisms" against intra-specific aggression. So rivalry leads invariably to violence and one violent act spirals into cycles of violent reprisals until finally the conflict fulfils itself in murder. One murder leads to cycles of reciprocal killings that form an unending series of revenge murders for so long as the killings continue to hold the same retaliatory meaning for both groups. The only way to put an end to the cycles of uncontrolled violence, asserts Girard, is through a final killing of a random victim whose guilt for all previous violence can be agreed upon by all warring parties.

The selection of the victim is entirely arbitrary and spontaneous. Yet the victim will always meet certain qualifications. He will be a recognizable surrogate for a guilty party so that he makes a believable "real culprit" for "just" punishment. But he will also be entirely vulnerable—without familial resources or social allies to champion his innocence or avenge his murder. Once unanimous agreement establishes the guilt of the surrogate for the previous social disruption, the victim will be treated as a criminal, denounced publicly, insulted, humiliated, beaten and whipped, and finally murdered (or symbolically murdered through expulsion from the community). The murder draws the community together and seals its unity in blood. Because the murder has a finality that brings the cycles of violence to a halt, the community can witness directly and immediately the "goodness" of their act manifest in their renewed communal integrity.

One of the most important (for our purposes) aspects of Girard's theory is his notion of "sacrificial crisis." Girard posits that, without the final murder, the violence in the community would reach endemic proportions in the form of a "sacrificial crisis," the worst form of the "bad" violence that operates without control or reason.[28] In a sacrificial crisis, tells Girard, cycles of reciprocal violence wear away the differences that distinguish individuals, both within families and within the community at large. Identities lose their meanings. Enemy cannot be separated from friend, family from stranger; not even the blood spilt for ritual and that spilt for criminal purposes can be differentiated. This is a crisis for the community because the cultural framework of a society is nothing but a regulated system of distinctions that permits the founding of identities, an existential space wherein private and social selves may be carved out. Where rituals of violence cease to regulate the rivalries and keep the identities of the rivals distinct, conceptual "order" collapses, meanings are lost and the social structure topples. Girard cites a famous passage from Empedocles' *Purifications* as an example of a sacrificial crisis:

> Father lifts up his own dear son, his form changed, and, praying, slays him—witless fool; and the people are distracted as they sacrifice the imploring victim, and he, deaf to its cries, slays it and makes ready in his halls an evil feast; and likewise son seizes father and children their mother, tearing out the life and eating the flesh of their dear ones. [29]

The sacrificial crisis can be averted by the "good" violence of ritual that focuses murderous rivalries on a surrogate victim bereft of the social resources to permit revenge. The only risk remaining then is that the innocent victim will be recognized *as innocent* and the fiction of the "justice" that brought closure to the violence will be revealed. To acknowledge the murder as the "dark deed" that it is, to admit the arbitrariness of the victim, would plunge the community back into the spiraling horror. Therefore, in the aftermath of the murder, all memory of rivalry and rejection must be erased, and the beneficial consequences of the murder retained, if the ritual is to prove successful in halting the spiraling violences. This is the task of religion, according to Girard's theory. Religious ritual transforms the surrogate victim into a collaborating participant, collapsing the evil "monstrous double" into self-sacrificing savior. The victim, demonized and murdered, is now exalted and divinized, and the beneficial effects of the murder (renewed peace and unity in the community) become visible proofs of the generosity and favour of the god.

Interestingly, the aspect of sacrificial ritual that led Girard to his theory was the stark polarity of the participants' responses to the victim, before and after the murder. Girard found it highly significant that the general loathing and disgust for the victim that precedes the murder (expressed in the insults, curses, and beatings) is replaced, once the deed has been accomplished, by articulations of gratitude, markedly venerating and adoring. The fact of this polarity leads Girard to the conclusion that ritual effects a "creative confusion" that produces dual social consequences: the loathed "monster" gives rise to the culture's prohibitions while the venerated "god" gives rise to the prescriptions that will hereafter (or until the next crisis) keep order in the community. In this symbolic transformation, monster becomes savior, ritual becomes myth, and communal atrocity becomes sacrosanct act rewarded by the blessings of the god. This "creative confusion" is so powerful a force, claims Girard, that all forms of cultural artifacts—linguistic, conceptual and symbolic—are generated from its vigor. Thus the human social, political and economic world arises.

Girard's tightly woven theory of the origin of the human world is unapologetically universalizing. Girard justifies this approach with the observation that the physiology of violence varies little across the human landscape, in methodology or effects.[30] Certainly one might argue that violence takes on infinite forms and continually evolves into new ways to humiliate and torture. Similarly, the uniformity of the experience of violation and responses to feeling violated are equally diverse, perhaps unique in every individual case.[31] Girard has contributed much to the contemporary debate on ritual's effects but his sweeping generalizations have, by far, been the greatest obstacle to his theory's general acceptance by the wider academic community.[32]

What is most disturbing to me about Girard's theory, however, is that the problem of violence and the measures called upon to solve that problem are essentially the same. Girard actually rallies the logic of polar oppositions to "order" the world's violences. Instead of exposing the falsity of simplistic moral polarizations, Girard reasserts ritual's logic in the ideological distinctions between "good" and "bad" violences. Furthermore, instead of collapsing the "religious worldview" that legitimates further violence, he promotes a revival of religious symbolism, especially Christian,[33] as a still-effective tool to disguise the murderousness of human worlds. Thus, Girard does not effect a philosophical response to the problem of violence. He does not call his reader to a self-examination for destructiveness so much as to a revival of the religious mechanisms that mask violence *as a problem* and mask religion itself as in collusion with violence.[34] In short, Girard's explanations of the origin of violence reaffirm the ritual ontologies, the over-simplistic, polarized understandings of the human world, that promote the facile moralizations that trigger pathologies of defense. Keeping religion's "dark secret" will ultimately elicit ritual's murderous responses to the differences encountered in the human world.[35]

The Consumptive and the "Rebounding"

Another important voice in the discourse on ritual is that of anthropologist Maurice Bloch. For Bloch, ritual has a primacy and a historical stability far beyond what experts have previously reckoned. Bloch's major works, *From Blessing to Violence* and *Prey into Hunter*, assert repeatedly the remarkable capacity of ritual to persist unaltered even where radical upheavals in belief systems or in politico-economic circumstances have uprooted and displaced entire social systems. Bloch's main contribution to the understanding of ritual, in my opinion, lies in his emphasis upon its endurance as the "logical infrastructure" of the social unit. Bloch sees that, while ritual is part and parcel of, and never isolated from, the socio-politico-economic world, it is the one feature of that world that can maintain intact throughout radical changes in these environing circumstances.

The reason for this remarkable resilience resides in what Bloch identifies as a minimal logical "core" to ritual. Evolving historical socio-politico-economic forms are related to the ritual process through this simple irreducible "core" as elaborations of it. In other words, ritual's ontological and ideological messages come to expression in the historical forms (political, economic and social) that arise to elaborate them. This logical "core" is, for Bloch, "quasi-universal" across the spectrum of ritual and religious practices, and constitutes "a permanent framework which transcends the natural transformative process of birth, growth, reproduction, ageing and death."[36]

Bloch demonstrates, through careful analyses of a range of past and present cultural groups, that rituals dramatize alternating episodes of social chaos and violent retribution. These polar episodes, so meaningful for Girard's account, dramatize, in Bloch's theory, a dialectic of domination and repression that communicates to the participants a duality in the living world, a duality that maintains between dead ancestral spirit and live tribal member, between animal and human, between men and women, and between old and young. The violent episodes that comprise the rituals, by juxtaposing the dual aspects of things, affirm the necessity and the efficacy of violence in unifying the two realms of existence. Violence manifests the influx of power from the eternal supermundane realm into the everyday. Rituals, therefore, communicate to participants that violence is rejuvenating, purifying and restorative.

The alternating episodes of ritual assume a rigid patterning that informs the life patterns of the social group. This patterning Bloch maps out in his account of the circumcision ritual of the Merina tribe of Madagascar. The ritual is initiated with an incident of disorder; some sort of indignity or violence is perpetrated by one segment of the society upon another. The violation may be simply the theft of corn or fruit from tribal fellows or neighbours, or it may entail more serious brutalizations. Members may whip, humiliate or even torture other fellows of their tribe. In the next episode, the victims turn upon their attackers, humiliating and beating them in turn. The frenzy of the violent sequences mounts until someone (or some group) becomes marked off as unassimilable, that is, unresponsive to the retributions meant to order the rebellious. The ritual reaches its climax in the murder of the unassimilable one(s). The murder may be real or metaphorical. That is, it may comprise a physical mutilation that effects a "death" of consciousness and "rebirth" as an adult member of the tribe, or it may comprise an expulsion from the tribe. However, insists Bloch, the occasional real murder is necessary to maintain the seriousness of the event.

A common feature of ritual noted by Bloch is that subordinates of the society (women and children) generally assume the early role of dominance in the ritual, beating or humiliating their social superiors. This stage, explains Bloch, enacts the breakdown of the social unit, dramatizing the chaos that ensues when the "rightful form" of the society is lost or abandoned. Violence spirals into retaliatory violence until a final bloody climax occurs—a murder or brutal mutilation that brings the chaos to a sudden halt. This radical act imposes order on the unit, returns the subordinate to their rightful places (on the bottom of the social heap) and reestablishes the "sacred" hierarchy of domination ordained by the ancestors and the gods. All take part in the closing festivities, reaffirming and celebrating the status quo of social relations. The dancing, singing, drunkenness and distribution of meats communicate to all that success is guaranteed for the tribe when all take their rightful places in the social order.

Rituals confirm the "rightness" of ordered systems by communicating what Bloch calls a "logic of domination." Such rituals have profound historical significance, asserts Bloch. They are highly conservative and inflexible precisely because they articulate, through their reciprocal exchanges, a fictional fluidity to the dominating powers of the society. The rite communicates the illusional "truth" that each person in the social group has an opportunity over time to be ruled and also to rule. The ritual maintains the fiction that all have their turn at empowerment and, while it always returns the subordinate to their inferior positions, it provides the illusion that the oppressed members of the society actively and willingly participate in their own oppression, while awaiting their turn to dominate. In the meantime of their oppression, they can, ironically, bear their humiliation with pride because they are rightful participating members of a powerful social order and because it is their willing submission to the social order that preserves the strength, stability and longevity of the unit. Though, for nearly everyone participating in the ritual, their rightful turn at the role of dominator is entirely illusory, the fact of the celebratory closure to the ritual—the laughter, the dancing, the feasting—confirms the power and the legitimacy of the social order of which all members may be proud.

The ritual, then, masks the reality of the pure exploitation of subgroups (of women by men, of children by parents, of young men by tribal elders) upon which the social order rests. It is only with the adoption of the ritual as a state ceremony, asserts Bloch, that the full ideological significance of the ritual comes into view. In the ritual's confirmation of a collusion between inferiors and superiors, the willing submitter, while separating herself from the "unassimilable one(s)" that will need to be murdered, affirms her enthusiastic enrollment in a powerful, aggressive society that will, when internal order is achieved, ultimately turn outward to dominate and conquer neighbouring tribes.

Bloch attributes the uncanny persistence of ritual to the power of its unique symbolism to manipulate the "cultural imaginary" of the group. Rituals, Bloch explains, "compress" a whole body of dominant symbols—polar and contradictory—into durable, obsessively-structured sequences of dramatic episodes. Ritual's uniquely symbolic nature makes it a powerful medium for transmitting ontological paradigms and political ideologies. Bloch states:

> [R]itual does its ideological job and carries at its core a simple and general message which can be received and used [to effect and justify] almost any type of domination.[37]

Ritual's primary message is that internal violences are necessary and desirable because they "order" a society to ensure its strength and survival in the external world, a claim that could not perhaps stand if exposed to rational criticism. But communicated *performatively* this message reaches its audience "in a hazy, non-discursive world, isolated from events and argument."[38] Ritual performs the ideological work of re-subordinating the oppressed and reaffirming the status quo of the power relations, while relieving the latter of having to defend the logical precepts upon which legitimacy is based.

It is in his *Prey into Hunter* that Bloch best demonstrates the secondary ideological effects of ritual. Since the "quasi-universal" structural "core" of rituals communicates that dual realms of reality exist, the one empowered and elevated by "consuming" the vitality of the other, ritual enacts the many phases of a "rebounding violence" that fulfills itself, in the final festivities, in a final externally-directed, cathartic dissemination. In the festival closure, a newly unified, rejuvenated, supermundane community turns its tribal aggressions upon external peoples. Often, rituals end with curses and insults flung at surrounding villages. There may be stone-throwing or a menacing removal of boundary stones. These threatening climaxes to the ritual convince Bloch that rituals provide an "idiom of conquest" (or consumption) that situates the tribe for aggressive extraterritorialization. Far from the "good violence" of Girard's account that remains effectively bound within ritual's strict regulatory margins, for Bloch violence always tends toward the overflow of ritual bounds. This is because rituals are ontological and ideological communications—"religious" truth. And religion is triumphalist in structure. Bloch states:

> [R]eligion so easily furnishes an idiom of expansionist violence to people in a whole range of societies, an idiom which, under certain circumstances, becomes a legitimation for actual violence.[39]

Bloch demonstrates once again how the "idiom of conquest" is effected, in his description of the initiation ritual of the Orokaiva tribe of Papua, New Guinea, a people unique for their maintaining a familial relationship with another species—the pig.

To fully appreciate the significance of the brutal climax of this ritual, it is necessary to understand the unique relations that this tribe maintains with its pigs. Pigs are raised as surrogate children, suckled alongside their human brothers, played with as siblings and lodged under the family dwelling. This social fact heightens the irony and the pathos of the violences enacted in the initiation ceremony. In the first stages of the ritual, children of the village are chased about, beaten and terrified by an "outside group" (masked tribesmen representing the dead ancestors of the tribe). In this episode of the drama, the children are hunted "like pigs" to the chanting of "Bite, bite, bite!" They are chased onto the very platform where pigs are traditionally slaughtered at festivals. There, they are rounded up like animals by these strange intruders and herded off to the woods. As frightening as this episode must be to the children, they are expected to cooperate with the attack, just as their parents, screaming and wailing at their children's plight, are expected to deliver over their young to the spirit strangers.

This first stage of the ritual Bloch calls a drama of penetration (conquest or consumption). In the woods, the boys are symbolically killed—locked in darkened huts, deprived of sight and sound. In this new "dead" state, they are fed strange foods, given new voices (taught to play the sacred flutes and bull-roarers that represent the voices of the spirits) and taught spirit dances. After a considerable time of seclusion, the youths are returned to the village, but this time not as

prey but as hunters. Having survived their "death" and the malice of the ancestors and the gods, the children are "reborn" as powerful adult members of the
tribe—elevated, transformed beyond the mere human, purified by terror and
pain, sanctified by contact with the transcendent, eternal realm.

The hunters immediately, upon re-entry to the village, express their newly
magnified power by throwing themselves in pursuit of the pig-children, the animal brothers amongst whom they were suckled and raised. The hunters become
warriors, perform a triumphant dance, sing the spirit-songs, and then, in a frenzy
of self-fulfillment, slaughter their pig-siblings, before their wailing (pig and human) mothers. The mourning is utterly genuine, insists Bloch, for the mothers as
much as for the hunter-brothers. For the latter, the slaughter is paradoxically
"both a glorious fulfillment of their destiny and a moment of real sadness."[40]

The slaughter and mourning is followed by the usual festivities—the songs
of triumph, the dances, the distribution of meats. But, as with the Merina, the
violence does not end here. The ritual culminates in gestures of communal aggression toward neighbouring peoples. In this closing drama, the entire village
participates in the removal of the peace-keeping boundary stones surrounding
the village. They volley provocative threats and curses at the external world.
These gestures of tribal aggressiveness symbolize the renewed vigor brought to
the tribe by the newly elevated warriors. But that aggressiveness is not merely
metaphorical. It is meant as an open-ended menace to outsiders and often comprises the beginning of real hostilities with neighbours.

Bloch posits as "quasi-universal" the ideological core of ritual that asserts a
"logic of domination" within the social structure and provides an "idiom of conquest" that often overflows or "rebounds" in violence toward the external world.
Bloch demonstrates the pervasiveness of the violent overflow structure of ritual
by applying his theory to a range of diverse cultural contexts: ancient Greek
ritual practices, biblical sacrifice stories, and current traditions of the Dinkas of
the Sudan and the Buid of Mindoro. In this broad survey, Bloch emphasizes
resonances of the consumptive idiom and the "logic of domination" and he notes
their function as ideological links between religious belief and political/military
aggressiveness. Bloch believes the spiraling violences in each of these cases to
express the escalating power believed transferred from a permanent transcendent
realm to the mundane world. Rebounding violences, rigid social structuring,
firm patterns of dominance and oppression, and aggressions toward external
peoples, claims Bloch, are consistent with a worldview bifurcated between the
exaggerated chaotic vitality of the everyday and a permanent stable order that
serves as a power-source maintaining the former.

Bloch's theory of ritual, like Girard's, emphasizes the necessity of marginal
beings (pharmakon, pigs, neighbours) as objects of aggressive focus to ensure
unity and self-definition within the social group. The slaughter of the innocent
alien and the subsequent distribution of meats is decisive in the formation of the
political alliances and networks of exchange that structure the societies. If Bloch
adds anything new to the understanding of ritual, it is the remarkable discovery
that sometimes rituals compress and convey ideologies that are not merely ab-

sorbed unconsciously by participants, but may be fully understood, knowingly executed, and willingly participated in.

The Enraged Mourner

The final account of ritual that I shall consider is that of anthropologist Renato Rosaldo, author of *Ilongot Headhunting 1883-1974: A Study in Society and History* and many articles on history, narrative and ethnography. Rosaldo lived for years among the Ilongot headhunting tribe, so his testimony bears a concreteness that contrasts curiously with the previous theories, compiled second-hand, as it were, from social-scientific data. There is a refreshing lack of sweeping generalization in Rosaldo's discussion of ritual, yet his lived experiences enable him to respond thoughtfully to the major theorists with specific corroborations or counter-evidence.

Rosaldo opposes Girard's claims of "mimetic desire" as the *sole* motivator of violence with the fact that violence sometimes has nothing at all to do with rivalry. One of the most commonplace and impassioned forms of violence, he explains, stems from the uncontrollable anger that arises at the sheer futility and absurdity of human tragedy. In headhunting societies, situations of devastating loss, like the illness or death of a loved one, do not simply culminate in the sadness and sense of loss we think stereotypical of mourning processes. For the headhunter, explains Rosaldo, there is rage in loss. The enraged one says, "I need a place to carry my anger." So the man or a group of men will embark upon a headhunting expedition, victimizing anyone who randomly falls in his/their path. There is absolutely no significance given to the victim. He is not creatively confused with the source of the rage. He becomes no god, no demon, no monster. Nor is the slightest significance given to the victim's head. It is simply thrown away once it has been taken. There is no anxiety, guilt or remorse for the crime experienced or expressed before, during or after the event. The headhunters speak in retrospect about the murder as a simple "letting-go" of their rage.

However, Rosaldo cannot deny that one factor of his lived experience remains resonant with the other theorists' accounts of ritual. Through the ritual of headhunting, violence is communicated as a powerful revitalizing mechanism that renews order and stability to individual and communal life in times of distress. Rage releases the power of violence and violence purifies. It clears the existential site, as it were, of the debilitating psychic debris that might otherwise paralyze action and immobilize the community. The taking of the head of a live victim is experienced as the ultimate act of violence. For this reason, it is highly purgative and "enormously productive...a source of vitality and energy. It motivates action—a key thing in their particular society."[41]

The headhunters' unique form of ritual violence, a most brutal and bloody form of murder, is understood by the participants as an entirely legitimate and effective means of recuperating natural loss and returning individual and communal life to stable coherence. Thus headhunting serves a crucial centralizing, unifying, and self-defining function in groups like the Ilongot.

Notes

1. "The Temptation of Temptation" in Emmanuel Levinas. *Nine Talmudic Readings.* tr. Annette Aronowicz. Bloomington: Indiana University Press, 1990. 30-50. 37.

2. F. Dostoevsky. *The Brothers Karamazov.* 298.

3. See Walter Burkert. *Creation of the Sacred: Tracks of Biology in Early Religions.* Cambridge, Mass.: Harvard University Press, 1996. 18-19.

4. W. Burkert. "The Problem of Ritual Killing" in *Violent Origins.* 147-176. 153.

5. One need not go so far as some behaviorists in accepting the postulation that a "violent gene" exists in the human being's biological composition, programmed by millennia of practice of murderous traditions. This is not a speculation that could ever bear substantiating proof. However, if it could be proven, it would offer a viable explanation for the otherwise inexplicable ability of individuals to, conscience-free, take part in the brutalizing activities of oppressive regimes, or even to stand by, apathetic, while their neighbours are brutalized.

6. In *Life or Death: Ethics and Options.* London: D.H. Labby, 1968. xxx.

7. First published in Austria as *Das Sogenannte Böse: Zur Naturgeschichte der Aggression* (1963). Published as *On Aggression.* tr. Marjorie Kerr Wilson. New York: Brace & World. 1966.

8. For example, Rollo May cites Lorenz's work as typical of the "general failure of biological approaches" to explain violence in human beings. He opposes Lorenz's account precisely on the argument that humans are different from animals. May's general thesis, however, is not opposed to my own. According to May, it is because humans create and interact through *symbols* and become obsessively wedded to those symbols that they are the cruelest species on earth. (*Power and Innocence.* New York: Norton & Co., 1972). 156.

9. See K. Lorenz. *On Aggression.* Chapter 3.

10. Lorenz. *On Aggression.* 239.

11. Lorenz. *On Aggression.* 42. c.f. 40.

12. Lorenz. *On Aggression.* 170-171.

13. Lorenz. *On Aggression.* 214. c.f.173. The primacy of aggression to love may explain the vital intimacy that psychologists assert between love and hate, an intimacy empirically evident yet counterintuitive to most of us. Anthony Storr (*Human Aggression.* New York: Atheneum. 1968. 16) has noted that many of the physiological changes manifest in sexual arousal are identical to those of aggressive arousal.

14. Lorenz. *On Aggression.* 171-172, 269. Thus: 284-287.

15. For a comprehensive treatment of the history of the concept of "instinct" and an account of its fall from grace with the scientific community, see Charles Burke. *Aggression in Man.* Secaucus, N.J.: Lyle & Stuart Inc., 1975. Burke explains that, since psychologists could quite successfully conduct research without the language of "instincts," avoiding that language relieved them of the task of analyzing the term as a concept, a task difficult if not impossible to achieve with lucidity.

16. Lorenz. *On Aggression.* 237.

17. Burkert. *Creation of the Sacred.* 18-19.

18. Burkert. *Creation of the Sacred.* 22.

19. Burkert. *Creation of the Sacred.* 29.

20. Burkert. *Creation of the Sacred.* 29.

21. For a comprehensive account of this theory, see first 80 pages of Walter Burkert. *Homo Necans: An Anthropology of Ancient Greek Sacrificial Ritual and Myth..* Peter Bing, tr. Berkeley: University of California Press, 1979.

22. Burkert. *Homo Necans.* 29-30.

23. Burkert. *Creation of the Sacred.* 33.

24. Girard. *Violence and the Sacred.* 300.

25. Girard. *Violence and the Sacred.* 299-300.

26. Girard. *Violence and the Sacred.* 240-243.

27. Girard's theory of mimetic desire draws from and maintains a striking resemblance to Freud's Oedipus complex. Freud was the first to see conflict as the determining socializing mechanism. But there are also irreconcilable differences between their theories. In Girard, Freud's "father" can be any model or rival; Freud's "mother" can be any desired object. Freud's "unconscious" becomes, in Girard, the "mythic mentality." (See *Violence and the Sacred.* 201 ff.)

28. Girard. *Violence and the Sacred.* 46.

29. Sextus. *Adv. Math.* IX. 129.

30. Girard. *Violence and the Sacred.* 47.

31. Emmanuel Levinas has argued persuasively in this vein. See "Transcendence and Evil" in *Collected Philosophical Papers.* 175-186.

32. See R.G. Hamerton-Kelly, ed. *Violent Origins.* 106-145. c.f. "Anthropological Commentary" by Renato Rosaldo. 239-244.

33. See Girard. *Things Hidden Since the Foundation of the World.* tr. Steven Bann, Michael Metteer. Stanford, CA.: Stanford University Press, 1987.

34. Religions remain themselves integrally entangled in the problem of violence in human communities. With their obsessive rules and regulations and their excessive seriousness, with their polarized over-simplified worldview, they help believers to maintain the dangerous fiction that violence is "good" if enacted by the legitimate authorities.

35. One might wonder, if Girard is convinced by his own theory, why he chooses to expose the "dark secret" about religion, when the stability and perhaps the continuance of our social systems is at stake in that exposure? Girard claims that exposure is now safe because Westerners no longer suffer from the "mythic mentality" that conceals the endemic rivalry of "mimetic desire." In modernity, he claims, legal systems substitute for religion's answers to the problem of violence, providing a fresh illusion of vengeful reciprocity to satisfy the offended. On the question of Westerners' freedom from the mythic mentality, see Richard Stivers. *Evil in Modern Myth and Ritual.* Girard promotes religious remedies to the problem of violence because he foresees that, as public confidence in the state's ability to render justice erodes and collapses into cynicism, a belated "sacrificial crisis" threatens renewed violence at every level of human society. He counsels that the Christian god who doubles as surrogate victim can forestall the crisis. For a less confident view of religion's effects, see Carol Lowery Delaney. *Abraham On Trial.* Princeton and Oxford: Princeton Paperbacks, 1998; *Disruptive Religion: The Force of Faith in Social Movement Activism.* ed. Christian Smith. New York and London: Routledge, 1996; Marc H. Ellis. *Unholy Alliance: Religion and Atrocity in Our Time.* Minneapolis: Fortress Press, 1997; James A. Haught. *Holy Hatred: Religious Conflicts of the Nineties.*

Amherst, N.Y.: Prometheus Books, 1995; Mark Juergensmeyer. *Terror in the Mind of God.* Berkeley: University of California Press, 2000.

36.Maurice Bloch. *Prey into Hunter: The Politics of Religious Experience.* Cambridge: Cambridge University Press, 1992. 3.

37. Bloch. *From Blessing to Violence.* 195.

38. Bloch. *From Blessing to Violence.* 195.

39. Bloch. *From Blessing to Violence.*6.

40. Bloch. *From Blessing to Violence.* 12.

41. See Rosaldo's concluding essay, "Anthropological Commentary" in ed. R. G. Hamerton-Kelly. *Violent Origins* 239-256. c.f. *Ilongot Headhunting 1885-1974: A Study in Society and History.* Stanford, California: Stanford University Press, 1980.

Chapter 3

Resonances in Ritual Theory

The prominent theorists on ritual that I have treated in the previous chapter hail from differing disciplines that function from diverse inductive bases, and thus they approach the subject from varying perspectives, employing varying methods of inquiry. This fact makes it all the more compelling that there are many correspondences among their claims, many "resonances" that link their theories.

By far the most common feature among the theories is the agreement regarding the fundamentality and primacy of experiential tradition over its conceptual/linguistic articulations—the priority of ritual over myth. Another point of univocity among the theories resides in the claim of the pervasiveness of rituals of violence (human and animal sacrifice, mutilations and tortures, expulsions) in early human communities and the primal nature of these bloody rituals with regard to rituals of nurturance, welcome, friendship and love.[1]

These experts also agree that violent rituals have, historically, been employed to serve two crucial functions in the social group: they have proven a highly effective means of ordering and stabilizing communities in times of unrest and of carving out self-identity for individuals and communities. The experts also concur in the claim that these important functions of self-definition and communal integrity are achieved with a high degree of success because of the ontological and ideological messages communicated through the events. Rituals conveyed worldviews and patterns of "natural" domination and oppression. They also taught that radical acts of violence are purifying to the group (or individual), drawing the power of the ancestors and the gods into the temporal realm to purge contaminating forces that seep from the chaotic external world into the sacred homespace.[2]

These prominent accounts of ritual theory demonstrate that rituals of radical violence either explicitly or implicitly communicate to participants who they culturally and individually are. They carve out self-identity for the social group by separating the belonging off from who they are not, "demonizing" the differ-

31

ent as threatening and powerful, and then murdering (or metaphorically murdering) it. Ritual configured difference as exaggeratedly potent, malevolent, and coercive while sameness was dramatized as unqualifiedly "good," safe and clean.

Violent rituals made clear the "we who belong" over against the "they that do not." They effected an illusion of clear, firm identity for the homespace by a radical over-simplification and polarization of phenomena. The unambiguous configuring of reality that comprises the "religious worldview" made the chaos of existence less chaotic, posited moral exemplars that were readily recognizable, and thus made moral choices easier in the everyday life of the group. They conferred upon the homespace a sense of "righteousness" and inviolability since its traditional practices—its values, virtues and social rituals—were ordained and sanctioned by the gods.

Archaic rituals played out episodes of violent exchanges between subgroups of the community, exchanges that caricatured the drama of human existence as a series of violent exchanges between competing powers. The violence culminated in the ritual murder, often a climax of pain and terror for the participants as much as for the victim. That final extreme violence fulfilled itself in festivity, and thus is violence theatricalized as beneficial and sanctifying, through reconnecting the group to the ancestors and the gods. The benefits of extreme violence could be immediately witnessed in the festival celebration and the distribution of meats. Differences that had previously interceded between members of the community and had caused local discord and rivalry could be perceived once again as minimal by comparison to the differences embodied in the "unassimilable" ones who had been expelled or murdered (and dissonance could be seen as unprofitable and unwise in the light of the recent fate of the non-belonging).

For these theorists, it is violence that energizes each episode of the ritual drama, violence that establishes the "rightful" ranking in the society, and violence that re-affirms the politico-social order and rejuvenates the group as a unified and discrete entity. It is violence that gives rise to laws and other social codes, political and social organizations and patterns of exchange. It is violence that brings festivity and peace. It is violence that "teaches" the young of each successive generation the cultural "truths" of the group. And it is violence that makes men of boys, loyal citizens of rebels, cooperative subgroups of the oppressed, legitimate rulers of oppressors. In short, it is violence that invigorates the homespace by drawing power from another permanent transcendent realm to purge contaminating forces and undesirable elements from the homesite and restore psychic balance and uniformity to the community of the belonging.

The radically simplified, polarized ontological vision, often called a "religious worldview," that these stark definitions schematized in the mental universe of the group concomitantly promoted uncompromising beliefs regarding appropriate values and behaviors. The ideals of integrity, unity, and consonance would be valued over multivocity and discord. Loyalty to the homespace and courage in confrontation with the alien would comprise the prescribed virtues—prescriptions that clearly configured "goodness" on the basis of identity rather than objective moral worth. This probably explains the dual function served by Athena, patron goddess of Athens. To fulfill the historical vision of homely virtues, she needed to comprise a force of understanding and of bellicosity. She had to be both the goddess of wisdom and the goddess of war. Similarly, on the level of the polis, the "just city" required guardians who served the double role of protecting friends and menacing enemies. On the grander social level, these dual aspects of "goodness" probably also explain how the Hellenes, though broadly diverse within their group (Sparta and Athens were radically different cities with opposing constitutions, values and ways of life), could form a cohesive entity when they found themselves confronted by non-Greek "*barbaroi*" (from which term we derive the word barbarians). The Greeks were able to put aside their petty internal differences whenever they saw the need to come together as an allied community to face a common enemy (like Persia).

Violent rituals legitimated violence on the (sometimes implicit, sometimes explicit) argument that existence is naturally chaotic and requires its ordering force. Where violence is configured as a manifestation of the sacred, both a symbol of divine presence among people and a gift from beneficent gods, it is difficult to see how any act of brutality, however extreme, however unwarranted, however destructive, could fail to be seen as legitimate, sanctified, necessary and desirable, if committed by the "rightful" authorities. Ritual violences, with their alternating episodes of insult, injury and murder, dramatically confirmed in the participants, through the pain inflicted upon their bodies and the terrors inflicted upon their psyches, a view of earthly existence as a dialectic of victimization and empowerment. They also initiated the participants into "pathologies of defense" that configured difference as exaggerated in power and malice and that counseled violent rejection of the alien for the sake of the purity and security of the homespace. The participants, themselves "purified" by ritual violence, often returned to the mundane with an "elevated" view of themselves. Having suffered and survived the torment of the demon or the malevolence of the spirit ancestors or gods, the initiated understood themselves as "chosen ones," ordained to protect the interests of the gods on earth and licensed to employ "good violence" to this end.

Obsessions with assertive identity need not be overly defensive and defensiveness need not be pathological. But where identity has been determined and the wisdom of defense has been taught through excruciating pain and terror, pathology is a likely result. The fact that defensive obsessions can readily "rebound" into offensive obsessions (as Bloch has indicated) illuminates the risk of obsessions per se. Obsessiveness, the definitive feature of ritual, signifies an over-seriousness with oneself and one's traditions, and an inflexibility that does not prepare people for the inevitable changes that life brings. Nor do obsessions with identity and defense prepare people for peaceful co-dwelling in a multi-cultural, multi-racial, multi-religioned world.

Many of the experts rallied here conclude with an ominous warning that, since violent rituals are primal and archaic (in the original multivocity of that Greek word[3]), dating back to the earliest human communities, it may be bloody murder, rather than lofty ideals and political astuteness, that underpin and configure the "civilizing processes" to which we so proudly credit the moral progress of the species. This paradox is concomitant to the paradox that motivates this inquiry: the coexistent yet morally irreconcilable facts of people's ideals of peaceful community and the bloody terrain of their actual engagement in the world.

Polar characterizations that rest upon clear and distinct definitions are the legacy of a violent human past of bloody sacrifice, physical torture, humiliation and mutilation. A "logic of domination" and an "idiom of conquest" may manifest a presence today in the rigidity of our "ordered" systems, their obsessive prescriptions and prohibitions of appropriate behaviors, in the seriousness with which we carve out inflexible self-definitions, in the sacredness that we attribute to our homespaces, and in the disgust and fear that we experience in the face of the alien. Pathologies of defense, scapegoat mechanisms, the humiliation of the outcast, the terror of the tormented, and the rage of the oppressed linger on in the founding logic and mechanisms of "order" that keep intact our systems, poising us aggressively in favour of "rebounding violences."

Violence remains an ineluctable element of orders per se. It is not difficult to see that the more "ordered" a society is, the more it conforms to the original structure established in ancient rituals of violence. The "order" of systems, however, is entirely illusional, grounded in perceived commonalities that deny individual differencing. This indicates that what matters is not so much commonality as *consciousness* of commonality. Perceived commonalities will always have a component of shared histories—shared memories of past triumphs or persecutions. To the degree that past victories or degradations become the focus of identity work, the group will be identity-obsessed and pathological. The more pathological the coalition, the greater the likelihood that stable identity will be sought through mechanisms of rejection that demonize the differences within and outside the group.

Thus we can say, as a general observation of their structure, that "ordered" worlds are metaphysically rapacious worlds that feed upon the marginal, the different, the alienated and the non-belonging. Ordering systems not only suppress and regulate violence; they comprise it and they compose it. Mechanisms of control and order and organization not only define the belonging and distinguish it from the marginal; they produce the alien through their alienating definitions. Prohibitions and prescriptions not only keep the differences within the system suppressed so as to produce an illusion of integrity and consonance; they increase the fear and sense of powerlessness from which burgeon hysterias for cleanliness. The different come to serve as horrifying objects of dread. They function as extreme derivatives that give boundaries and definition to a "human" world. Extremes of human difference serve to reconfirm the system and to reinstate the legitimacy of those who belong. Thus the non-belonging serve well in the identity work of the system, even as, paradoxically, they serve the self-defeating purpose of reconfirming as "rightful" the violences visited upon them.

We clearly need to address the problem of the faulty ideals of order and unified integrity that structure our ordered systems. We need to make changes in the way we think about difference and thus in the way we imagine commonalities. However, the theorists of ritual almost unanimously agree that changes are difficult, if not impossible, from within the logical and symbolic system of orientation. We are always already ideological prisoners of our systems of oppression, trapped within lifeworlds always already shaped by violence and ordered by pathologies of defense. Maurice Bloch echoes the other anthropologists when he asserts pessimistically:

> [G]iven the raw materials of our shared perceptions of the processes of life and with the limited tools of ritualization and metaphor at our disposal, the constructions of rebounding violence, in their many structural forms and contents, are the only way in which the necessary image of society as a transcendental and legitimate order can be constructed. This would... mean, therefore, that we cannot construct cosmologies other than those which would offer a toehold to the legitimation of dominance and violence.[4]

Notes

1. Rosaldo is the single exception to this consistency among the anthropologists surveyed here. He seems to suggest that, with the Ilongot, everyday family and community relations are loving and nurturing. Fathers often tend the children while the women work in the fields through the day. Headhunting only results in response to a break in the everyday equilibrium, when tragedy besets the group or an individual through illness or death of a loved one. See Rosaldo's concluding essay, "Anthropological Commentary" in *Violent Origins.* 239-256.

2. Again, Rosaldo is less committal regarding a "two-worlds" explanation of the violence in the case of the Ilongot head-hunting society. He suggests that radical violence is seen simply as a highly effective means of purging the rage that accompanies life's tragic losses.

3. Ἀρχή, from ἄρχομαι, to begin, to make a beginning of a thing, to rule, be leader of. Connected to *archon*, the name for ruler, captain, chief or king. The Archon was the chief magistrate of Athens.

4. Bloch. *Prey into Hunter.* 105.

Chapter 4

Mythical Traces of the
Legacy of Violence

under the shadow of the "fall"

The experts on ritual assure us that rituals endure through radical upheavals in historical circumstances. They persist through changing political and economic realities, and through radical transitions in belief systems and cosmological visions. The ritualized logic that structures our systems and is articulated in our myths and social codes can persist across ever new conceptual landscapes, and they have likely been persisting, according to these experts, since the early history of the species, perhaps even since Paleolithic times. It is the underlying logic, the enduring simplistic polarity by which we understand our worlds as "ordered" rather than "chaotic," that has been shaping our stories and our myths, and governing and restricting the role of creative freedom and fantasy from time out of historical mind.

I am not suggesting that all rituals are maladaptive or violent. Nor am I proposing that all human actions in all human societies, as a result of their violent ritual histories, have been destructive and devoid of value. There have been many superb humanitarian acts in the history of human achievement that testify to the ability of people and cultures to break free of their histories, to overcome innate dispositions and outsmart the governing logic of their languages and other institutions. Nor am I submitting that all our myths are harmful. On the contrary, it seems clear to me that our narrative histories comprise a prodigious power, and that power can be put to good use as readily as it can be put to destructive purposes. Stories, in the nursery and beyond, can shape patterns of behavior positively.

I am certain, however, that care must be taken with stories, that the fictional intake of youngsters needs to be regulated, that discussion must complement story-telling, that critical "work" must be part of their play. We must take special care with myths because, shrouded in a veil of illusion and masked by a frank admission of falsity, they can intimate to the careless listener a host of dangerous "truths." We can easily forget that, even where their falsity is frankly admitted, myths can maintain a hold over the symbols and connecting logic that compose the "common mental world" of a people. They can communicate a "logic of domination" that legitimates oppressions and counter-cultural rejections on the ideological argument that order and conformity are morally superior to difference and multiplicity of truths.

This chapter considers a few of the more frequent and prominent themes repeated in myths of the Western tradition. There are a few themes that strike the student of myth as pervasive of the mythological heritage of human beings across widely diverse cultural boundaries. First of all, origin myths, thought historically to be the most powerful stories since beginnings reveal the "true" character of things, usually posit the advent of humankind upon the cosmic scene after the power struggles have been decided. Radical acts of violence on the part of unambiguously "good" powers have brought to order a chaotic universe, plagued by monsters, demons and other hostile forces. Without these extreme violences (castrations of father gods, cruel deceptions by mother gods, powerful displays of cosmic might, secret craftings of bitter weapons that are turned upon kin), it is understood that chaos would maintain and monsters would still reign the universe.

Humans are generally depicted as favoured by the god(s) in the earliest scenes of the cosmic drama. But, very soon into the tale, a fall from grace (through a fateful alliance or some corruptness of their character) effects an alienation from the divine progenitors and a literal "fall" from the original paradisal home to a life of toil and hardship on a harsh, unforgiving planet. The myths are generally highly ambiguous as to who or what is the real cause of the fall, though corruptness of the species is almost always a contributing element. The listener is left to wonder: are the gods simply poor craftsmen who cannot get their creations right or are humans simply too ontologically flawed to keep divine company?

It is clear that the mythologem of "rightful powers" and their violent ordering mechanisms conveys almost intact the ritual "logic of domination" and its concomitant "idiom of conquest." These origin myths assert directly the power of violence to purify and order the chaotic. Violence is depicted as legitimate in the hands of legitimate authorities and a highly effective method of establishing "right" ordering. The mythologem of the "fall" of humankind from an original home will also have some definitive messages for the believer. It dictates a view of earthly existence as darkened—weary, toilsome, sorrowful, unstable, painful and deathly—especially by comparison with the paradisal home of human origin—permanent, deathless, joyful, transcendent to the chaos of life. The understanding of the "human condition" that stems from this mythologem depicts human beings as "homeless," abandoned to a hostile alien setting (instead of an earthly "home" that ought be cherished), unworthy of the gods' love, and yet unclear about the justice of that fate. Under this darkened view, human existence on earth is rendered tragic.

The tragic bearing of many origin myths, from ancient Mesopotamian to Greek to Judeo-Christian, suggests that those raised in traditions promoting such tales as religious fact may inherit a sense of guilt (as members of a corrupt species), and feelings of victimization (at the harsh treatment of vengeful gods) and an outlook of powerlessness (against a cruel fate decided long before their time). I shall call this orientation an "existential of nostalgia" to underscore its tragic bearing and the sense of loss that inheres in the self-definition of those under its unhealthy thrall. I suspect that where people are oriented nostalgically, they may be resentful of their human state. Perceiving it as disordered and degraded, they may feel impotent, insecure, morally confused and overly defensive, the very conditions that are likely to trigger "pathologies of defense" and recall the mythical "cures" for disorder and contamination (violent "ordering mechanisms").

This is not to assert that people raised within the religious worldview are more overtly violent people. But they do maintain the bifurcated polarized ontology, the "two-worlds" view that can sanction "ordering" violences upon a "fallen" world. The religious may tend to assert themselves more vehemently, more obsessively, more self-righteously, into the ordering of their "alien" homes. The dangerous ontologies and tragic mythologems may rest quiescent in their "common mental world," shaping their vision of reality and inclining them tragically toward earthly life. The ontological and ideological messages of religious myth may be festering beneath a surface of calm, silent and unobservable yet lingering until situations of disorder or peril call forth the immense restorative powers prescribed by the latent paradigms.[1]

The themes that may breed an "existential of nostalgia" and those that prescribe the mythical cures for that disordered condition (violent "ordering" strategies for self-definition and integration) are pervasive of the narrative history of the West and comprise a curious connecting thread between the religious, the cosmological and the philosophical myths that provide the conceptual and narrative ground of Western civilization. There is frequent repetition of these themes throughout Hesiod, whose works held great weight in the ancient and classical Greek world. His view of reality expresses the general orientation of the average Greek up until Zeus became so powerful that he eclipsed the other gods, stepped down from Olympus and came to be nailed on a cross. We find the themes of human corruption and the consequent fall from grace, and spectacular demonstrations of the violent "ordering mechanisms" throughout Empedocles' two proems, *On Nature* and *Purifications*. These are parallel tales that track human corruption, as it were, from above (in the god's-eye view of cosmological discourse) and from below (a recipe for re-elevation from the point of view of the "fallen"). Plato's retelling of the old origin myth in the

Statesman parallels Hesiod's in most respects but it offers a single optimistic benefit over Hesiod's account. He has Socrates ask (at 272bc) regarding the golden age men:

> Did the [golden men] use all these advantages [of peace and leisure] to promote philosophical inquiry? As they associated with one another and with the animals, did they seek to learn from each several tribe of creatures whether its special faculties enabled it to apprehend some distinctive truth not available to the rest which it could bring as its contribution to swell the common treasure store of wisdom? If they really did all this it is easy to decide that the happiness of the men of that era was a thousandfold greater than ours. But if, when they had taken their fill of eating and drinking, the discussion they had with each other and with the animals were of the kind that the surviving stories make them out to have been, then, according to my judgment at any rate, it is equally clear what our verdict must be.

Plato's suggestion here is that leisure and peace are all very well, if they are put to good philosophical use, but, if not, then humans are better off under the stimuli of toil and suffering, struggling against the chaos to search out their wisdom and forge friendly associations and communications across the diverse landscape of earthly existence. I believe that closing the old tale with this new hopeful twist (that suggests the "good life" may be carved out even on a harsh earth if appropriate philosophical methods are employed) countervails against the tragic incline of the old myth.

The tragic themes and ordering cures echo through Genesis' dual creation accounts. God, the wholly good power, with a blast of his omnipotent word, banishes a dark and menacing Chaos and brings to ordered existence all beings in the universe. When the first humans disappoint the god, they are thrown from paradise to struggle against the elements, bear their children in pain, murder their brothers and swindle their fathers, enslave their neighbours and slaughter their enemies. With this "fall," reality splits into two worlds: one chaotic, brutal and wretched, the other stable, peaceful and transcendent. Superior might is the identifying mark of the good. Is it any wonder then that the first humans, tossed to the elements to wander homeless and godless, "rebound" violently against their brothers and their neighbours, generation after generation?[2]

Given the brutal techniques by which Christian evangels brought the word of god to heathens on both sides of the Atlantic, and of Muslim zealots as they brought northern and eastern Africa under the god's law, and the state of Israel today as it guns down schoolchildren and massacres people at prayer in its "holy land," there is good reason to suspect that the world's three "great religions" are all infected by the "logic of domination" and its "idiom of conquest." The separate but equally bloody histories of the sibling religions spawned from Abraham[3] suggest a common logic of self-righteous domination, despite the cultural and religious differences that divide them. The fact that these religions have been brothers in parallel histories of murderous evangelism has not prevented a Cain-like animosity from piloting their brotherly interactions with each other.

Present-day cultures emerge from their ritual histories under the burden of particularly violent ideologies, according to many of the experts. The performative traditions have come to expression in a configuration of mythical themes particularly tragic and violence-legitimating. The myths demonstrate conceptually what is already at work at a pre-conceptual level, in the bodily dispositions and psychic inclinations of the cultures emanating from these narrative histories. They illustrate a bifurcated, starkly polarized and simplistic view of reality wherein forces are clearly and distinctly "good" and "bad" and where moral decisions are easy. Given the messages communicated through our myths, it is reasonable to suspect that a sense of "fallenness," lostness and alienation may linger in our psyches. Guilt, resentment, confusion and a sense of human fragility and impotence may be integral to our view of mortal existence. If so, this would create a longing for belonging that would explain the current obsessions with identity that characterize not only the rich arrogant Western nations but generally typify conflicts across the globe today.

It is possible that the violence that characterizes the terrain of human engagement, and has always characterized human engagement throughout the long history of the species, is linked to and perhaps dictated by performative and conceptual histories. The consequent obsessiveness and over-seriousness with identity issues would only be exacerbated by the futility of efforts at intimacy in a cutthroat capitalist world. It may be the tragic sense of life, the "existential of nostalgia," that comes to be expressed in a society's general apathy toward its own political events and decisions and toward the plight of its own oppressed. Or tragic bearing may fix its moral attentions inward and manifest itself as obsessions with personal or national well-being and a consequent indifference toward the miseries of other nations, causing otherwise caring people to dismiss the starvation of African children or the bayoneting of Croatian babies as "not our concern."

The bloody history of the species, with its Crusades, Inquisitions, slave trades, conversions at gunpoint of entire continents, Holocausts, terrorisms, and its continuing apathy toward the wretchedness of our fellows, comprises compelling evidence that the messages compressed in ritual and articulated in myth continue to be lived out in subsequent centuries. They continue to define the different as demonic and thus to orient people pathologically with regard to their neighbours. They continue to marshal people according to ideals of integrity and unity, ideals that configure appropriate behaviors on the basis of identity rather than moral worth or worldly effects, and they continue to dispose people toward violent solutions to problems of unrest and dissonance.

Sociologist Neil Smelser asserts that Western cultures display all the telltale signs that myths sanctioning destructive behaviors "enjoy a more or less universal and permanent existence" in the psychic orientation of those cultures.[4] That sanctioning may not fulfill itself in overtly destructive behaviors, but may "be activated only under certain historical conditions."[5] Nevertheless, the disposition toward violence is there, claims Smelser, just beneath the surface of our everyday beneficences. It is there inclining our attitudes and our actions. It may be there orienting us in our view of alien others. Cultural myths, argues Smelser, help to bring people to the threshold of destructive behavior because they provide paradigms of valiant action, according to some ideal of heroic masculinity. Such paradigms legitimate violence as a viable and effective ordering strategy. The paradigms come to be re-expressed as cultural champions and fictional heroes like Superman and Lone Ranger. Typically, argues Smelser, the new ideal is a one-man vigilante who, by virtue of hypermasculine qualities and above all moral superiority, brings evil forces to a swift and harsh justice by stepping outside and above the law. It is difficult to gauge the magnitude of the effects of such paradigms in the lifeworld of a people, but Smelser is convinced that their influence is profound and he is pessimistic about their extirpation. He states:

> Many of the forces that go into the legitimization and rationalization of evil are firmly rooted in the depths of a man's impulse life, his social and political conflicts, his ideological and religious traditions and his situational vicissitudes. As a result, they are likely to be very impervious to modification by deliberate social policy.[6]

Modern societies, especially in the West, may think themselves free of their ritual/mythical histories. However, they still show all the signs of a dispositional allegiance to the "religious worldview." Western cultures share a tradition of value-ordering that is reflected in their systems of status stratification based on social values or religious criteria often connected to (falsely) glorified particularized histories or claims of a special relationship with the divine. Social identity is still constructed on the basis of these values. Social hierarchies related to expressive social and religious values permeate and regulate social and political institutions still today, though they can become functionally independent of political and economic circumstances. Even in the latter case, however, there persists the concern with relative degrees of purity and contamination. These may not find expression in the ritual terms that I am employing here, but may be interpreted in terms of special relationships with the god or in terms of "natural/unnatural" gradations of human being. The concern for purity can be manifest in pseudo-scientific notions of superiority grounded in social, racial, ethnic or religious differences.

Societies today, no matter how allegedly "democratic" or secularized, remain "religiously" structured value hierarchies. And value hierarchies are self-justifying and self-perpetuating. The patterns of belief within the system provide the justification for fixed internal structuring, legitimating its elevations and its oppressions, its patterns of dominance and suppression, as well as providing justification for wars with alien societies. Hierarchical systems are self-reinforcing, despite the fact that the oppressed often exist in numbers that would raise questions about their suppression. The cause of the persistence of oppressive systems, according to the social scientific community, is simple.[7] Ordered, ranked systems serve people's needs well. Human beings are prone to feelings of helplessness and dependency perhaps even more now, faced with the bewildering complexities of modern life, than in the days of the ritual hunt. They still require some effective means of ordering the confusing data of empirical experience and of establishing a sense of belonging in an alienating world. Systems order a person's thinking for her. Modern systems serve the same sorting processes that Burkert tells us served the Paleolithic hunters well: they arrange the confusing experiential data into those simple symbolic containers that sort meaningful "world" from the chaos of existence and make sense of individual lives.

Thus people, even those most oppressed by the system in which they live, often tend to internalize their differences, even the ethical conflicts they may have with regard to the system, so that they can, with minimal conflict, find a place of belonging and a live a "meaning-full" life within a stable organization of social significances. It is this general allegiance to system that explains the uncanny ability of the degraded and oppressed in a society to live otherwise happy and satisfying lives, despite the inequities of the system. It explains why people often readily opt for and even embrace the alienating aspects of their lives. It also explains the ability of otherwise caring individuals to go about their daily affairs with equanimity amidst the undeniable evidence of the suffering and wretchedness of their fellows, as long as the plight of the have-not's does not impinge directly upon their personal welfare. In most stable societies, now and in the history of human community, it is the ranked system of inequalities that is understood, by those on the bottom of the social ladder as much as by those at the top, to provide gratification of particular social needs and fulfillment of material expectations, and to regulate mutual obligations between the various spheres of social being.

The fact that the oppressed as much as the oppressors within a system willingly re-endorse the system demonstrates a curious fact about identity work as it is actually carried out in the world. It demonstrates that, within any society, there is a continual tension *within* social identity *between* belonging and alienation. This links to the fact that the commonalities upon which homogeneous identity is based are entirely illusional at the most allegedly stable of homespaces. Thus, the non-belonging are "alien" and "demonic" to the same degree of illusoriness that identities are "stable" and non-fluctuating. The "religious worldview" (even in its modern reformulations) still serves to keep the illusions in force and to keep their illusoriness concealed. Religion's collective representations can sanction behavior that is ethically indefensible, a fact that has been persuasively established by Mark Juergensmeyer, in his very important treatment of the global rise of religious violence, *Terror in the Mind of God*.[8] The development of symbols that legitimate force, and the logical connections that link those symbols, are ineradicable features of religious belief and these extend into myths of progress and notions of "natural" causality as well. Sanctioning forces that give license to oppressions and exaggeratedly aggressive behavior by the power nodes of the society are more easily accomplished where a "religious worldview" (even where secularized) remains intact.

Notes

1. James A. Haught closes his book *Holy Hatred: Religious Conflicts of the Nineties*: "Ironically, nations with fervent religion often have the worst social evils. For example, the United States has more churchgoing than any other major democracy, and it reports much higher rates of murder, rape, robbery, shootings, stabbings, drug use, unwed pregnancy and the like, as well as occasional tragedies such as those at Waco and Jonestown, Guyana. There may be no link between the two conditions, but the saturation of religion... [in] societies rife with fundamentalism and religious tribalisms are prone to sectarian violence. In contrast, England, Canada, Japan and such lands have very scant churchgoing, yet their people are more inclined to live peaceably in accord with the social contract." (232).

2. Perhaps the most dangerous of Biblical myths in the Judeo-Christian heritage is the story of Abraham's sacrifice of his son Isaac. This story is also highly significant because, as Abraham is considered the founding father of the three "great religions" of the West, its paradigmatic power is broad. It has been persuasively argued that the god's arbitrary demand that an innocent boy be slain, and the good Abraham's unquestioning compliance to this senseless violence has left an ethical legacy, a model for human behavior, that would have had powerful weight in molding the cultural imagination of the West. (See Carol Lowery Delaney. *Abraham On Trial*. Princeton, N. J.: Princeton University Press, 2000).

3. See note 2, this chapter.

4. Neil Smelser. "Some Determinants of Destructive Behavior" in William Henry, and Nevitt Sanford, eds. *Sanctions For Evil*. San Francisco: Jossey-Bass Inc., 1971. 15-24. 20.

5. Smelser. "Some Determinants." 20.

6. Smelser. "Some Determinants." 23.

7. For a clear and thorough treatment of this issue see George de Vos. "Conflict, Dominance and Exploitation" in *Sanctions For Evil*. 155-173.

8. Mark Juergensmeyer. *Terror in the Mind of God*. Berkeley, Calif.: University of California Press, 2000.

Chapter 5

Home-Craft in the
History of Philosophy

"innocent egoist and alone"

From Ritual to Myth to Philosophy

Thus far, in my effort to understand the gap between the benevolent intentions of individuals and the bloody terrain of their actual engagement in the world, I have considered the anthropologists' claims that historical forces have bequeathed to modernity dispositions and inclinations toward destructive behaviors. I have, on the basis of the anthropologists' theories of ritual, assumed that our social, political and economic systems have been shaped by, and remain logically consistent with, historical patterns of domination and suppression, patterns legitimating oppressions within systems and "rebounding" aggressions upon neighbours. I have assumed that the dangerous ontologies and ideologies linger in our narratives and I have thus mapped resonances of ritual's messages through Western myths.

Our ritual and mythical histories of violence seem to offer compelling explanations to the problem of human violence, both in modern times and throughout the history of the species. They also offer persuasive arguments for the "gap" between benevolent intentions and destructive engagement that motivates my project here. If, compressed within the logic upon which our systems are founded, there remain ontological and ideological messages legitimating, then, at a preconscious, pre-conceptual level (and perhaps under certain circumstances even at a conscious, conceptual level), our understanding of ourselves and our "civilizing" forces may remain shaped according to the archaic conviction that the homespace is inviolable and pure, yet constantly under threat of contamination by the alien.

The anthropologists' speculations also offer some interesting corollaries. We may deduce from their theories the further conjecture that, precisely by adhering to the very ideals that undergird our systems (integrity, order, unity), we may be heightening our propensity for violence and reconveying the logic created in the "murderous" rituals practiced by our earliest ancestors. Perhaps the very ways in which, today, we "find" ourselves as individuals and as social entities remain configured by mechanisms of rejection that conceptualize the different as exaggeratedly threatening and powerful—demonic.

To test this possibility, I shall consider the task of identity formation and consolidation as it has historically been presented by philosophers. Employing the metaphor of "home-craft" to designate the task of identity work, I shall seek signs of a propensity for violence at the homesite and intimations of a perceived purity and inviolability. First I shall reflect on Nietzsche's account of the task of home-craft as creative artistry, then I shall consider Plato's account of psychic consolidation as "justice." Next, by tracing the task of identity consolidation through the works of Husserl, then Heidegger, and finally Emmanuel Levinas, I shall offer a brief history of phenomenological accounts of the structure of our identity spaces and of the psychic mechanisms by which we carve out our "homes" in the world. I shall attempt to demonstrate, through these philosophers' accounts, "blind spots" that eclipse from the view of the subject its indebtedness to history in a prior constitution that gives "world." The subject's tunnel vision, obsessively focused upon the "now" of his project of existence, implies a concomitant ethical blindness that permits the subject a purified and innocent vision of the home territory, while also permitting strategies for living, however violent, to appear as justified and inevitable.

The reader will note undeniable resonances among the insights into home-craft discerned by these various philosophers, despite their diverse imagery and the differences in their philosophical approaches (let us call them idealistic, existential and phenomenological). This fact makes it all the more compelling that, from their differing angles upon the problem, analogous paradoxes emerge that consistently disclose tensions between the *lived* experience of free and spontaneous agency and the prior formulation of the subject as a product of history and world. A discomfiting reality will unfold through my treatment of these philosophers' accounts of home-craft. It will emerge into view that, from within the homespace, the subject's "egoisms," no matter how oppressive within homespaces or violational of environing others, are *lived* as *both* innocent and necessary strategies of a *heroic* "ontological adventure."

Nietzsche

In the trajectory of the violent rituals and tragic myths whose dangerous "truths" the anthropologists have said undergird our systems and institutions and our patterns of thought and action, "homeless" human beings, thrown to an alien and hostile earth, carve out their dwellings within material and existential sites, on multiple and simultaneous levels within intricate webs of interrelations. Home-craft, at its most primary level, is lived as a crafting of the self into a noble and worthy locale of existence through the application of "virtues" perceived as ideal. Friedrich Nietzsche describes succinctly this enterprise, as it is carried out at its most conscious level by those most obsessed by the task, effectively highlighting the creative and ascetic aspects of home-craft.

> *One thing is needful.* "Giving style" to one's character—a great and rare art! It is exercised by those who see all the strengths and weaknesses of their own natures and then comprehend them in an artistic plan until everything appears as art and reason and even weakness delights the eye. Here a large mass of second nature has been added; there a piece of original nature has been removed: both by long practice and daily labour. Here the ugly which could not be removed is hidden; there it has been reinterpreted and made sublime. . . . It will be the strong and domineering natures who enjoy their finest gaiety in such compulsion, in such constraint and perfection under a law of their own.[1]

This passage describes identity-formation as a "needful" active process proceeding according to conscious criteria that compose an "artistic plan." The passage also gestures toward the problem that accompanies the task in its most obsessive forms: home-craft can become a "compulsion" when practiced by "strong and domineering natures." It is governed *only* from within, limited *only* by inner "constraints" and personal principles of "perfection." That is, the "artistic plan" follows *only* "a law of [one's] own." Nietzsche's creative artist is autonomous and free, sculpting out the existential landscape according to entirely personal ideals.[2]

For Nietzsche, the feature that distinguishes the noble from the weak and decadent nature is the blunt honesty characteristic of the noble, an honesty that recognizes violence as necessary to order and, in fact, inevitable in the natural order of things. The noble person acts violently without false remorse, knowing that violence is the prerogative of the strong. It is the strong man's right and charge. The artist understands himself to be like life itself, operating through injury, insult, exploitation, and destruction, to bring about the most desirable *con*structions. He looks squarely at his violations and interprets them as "natural" and in any case inevitable—consistent with all events in the organic world. Violence is a necessary component of order. Pain and suffering, from the point of view of the one imposing them, is never a moral oversight—never "senseless." The artist's honesty about the state of nature and his refusal to take refuge in the moral illusions entertained by the weak makes the artist laudably "just."

Bad conscience about the necessary violences with which perfect worlds are carved out and heroic greatness is achieved, for Nietzsche, is an illness. The healthy are violent in act and bearing—consciously and joyously so—because, without guilt or remorse or moralizing apprehensions, they are involved in an artistic project. Artists are permitted, nay expected, to break norms! It is the crucial function of their craft that they "impose forms" upon the chaotic and barren. Nietzsche insists that artists cannot be limited by the petty social norms of lesser people. Rather, they know themselves "to be justified to all eternity in [their] works."[3]

That the artist feels "justified to all eternity" in his works exposes a deep sense of "rightness," innocence, inviolability, and "elevation" above the petty norms of the crowd. The conviction of this personal uprightness is bound up in the nature of his craft; the importance of his work purifies and elevates its effects above the moral concerns of lesser beings. His violences are justified (made "just") because enacted in the interest of a greater vision, beyond the trivial and the mundane.

In less strong and domineering natures, ordering their homespaces according to their (lesser) visions of perfection, the violence that is the "necessary component of order" and the mindful or incidental fallout of their artistry will be understood as equally necessary and inevitable. The less strong may be equally violent *where they can manage it* and, where they cannot, may construct decadent visions of perfection that make virtues of cowardice and subordination and grant recompense for weakness in a transcendent gift system. However, if Nietzsche is right, the less strong will not be less prone to violence but will be less honest about their violences, refusing to recognize them as such or suffering bad conscience after their events.

Plato

In Plato's account of the ordering of the soul, home-craft is also presented as a task of harmony and integration, and, in the *Republic*, the innocence, nay ideality, of the task is underscored by Socrates' designation of proper psychic ordering as the form of Justice itself. The project of organizing the self by integrating conflicting intellectual goals, appetitive desires, and impassioned loyalties mirrors the work of the orderly gods in the cosmos and, could it be successfully achieved by people, would manifest Justice itself in the realm of human existence.[4] The *Republic* offers a compelling model for integrated identity, ostensibly by applying only the gentle art of persuasion to order diverse internal parts. However, in the mirroring of the soul into the city, the soul *writ large*, a less gentle aspect of persuasion comes into view. We see that justice cannot be achieved in the city without definite violences—lies, deceptions and censorships visited by the power nodes of the society (philosopher-kings) upon their subordinates, and, curiously, *for their own good.*

The image of the soul in the *Republic* (and similarly in the *Phaedrus* and the *Timaeus*) homologizes the three portions of the soul to parts of the human body. According to this imagery, the soul/city/cosmos achieves a "natural" justice when the lofty citadel of the head/philosopher-king/divine craftsman (homologized as divine reason) commands and regulates the lesser, mere mortal parts: the appetites/commoners/random material forces of the cosmos (homologized as the stomach), and the passions/guardian warriors/heavenly forces (homologized as the heart). The stomach is the largest but lowliest of the parts, a constant threat to the order of the whole because its satisfactions are purely material and without intrinsic regulatory mechanisms. Hailing from ignoble stock, it is resistant to the demands of divine reason. The spirited part (the heart) serves at the bidding of the rational and provides the passion—and, in the imagery of the "watchdog," the loyalty and the muscle—to impose order among the diverse interests at play in the soul/city/cosmos.

Bruce Lincoln finds striking the resemblance between the tripartite image of the soul in the *Republic* and traditional Indo-European themes and imagery that, historically, served as the ideological apparatus to justify and support coercive and repressive social hierarchies in the Indo-European world.[5] The coercive persuasion that orders the "just city" and propagandizes for the rule of an elite rational deliberative group guided by transcendent realities and backed by the passionate muscle of the loyal noble element (the guardian warriors) mirrors the "persuasions" whereby priestly classes historically solidified their power and justified their dominance. Such myths asserted a "natural order" to the cosmos, configuring as "natural" and "right" the dominance of an elite group and justifying the oppressions they visited upon sub-groups. Homologizing myths propagandized that rule was a sacred prerogative of a special segment of the human order, ordained by the gods to perform a special function *for the good* of the whole society. Their dominance and oppressions were, through the myths, declared an ethical necessity encoded in the fundamental structure of reality, just as sure a necessity as the fact that bodies function best when the head, and not the stomach, is in control. Lincoln's treatment of homologizing paradigms that justify hierarchical ordering demonstrates persuasively that, not far behind any ideology of "natural" and "just" orders, no matter how lofty its guiding ideals, there generally lurks a state-sanctioned system of violences directed by elites and carried out by warrior henchmen.

However, violences internal to the system were not the only outlet for aggression available to the elites. In ancient elitist societies, oppressions within the system were often eclipsed (or justified) by hostilities directed toward the external world. Wars and raids on neighbours were a seasonal occupation of the soldiery and bore rich yield to the society in the form of slaves, agricultural produce and other booty. Unlike the possession-free guardians of Plato's "just state," however, the violences of the traditional hierarchical city tended toward the enriching of the aristocratic and priestly powers. The superiority of their lifestyles, their material dominance, offered visible proof that the gods favoured the upper classes. This in turn effectively reinforced the ideology of natural hierarchy. The commoners could readily recognize their own lowliness by comparison with the magisterial ways that warriors and priests lived. So warfare confirmed the rights of the dominant and confirmed in their subordinates a "false consciousness" that contributed to and reinforced the system that oppressed them.

Perhaps the *Republic* is correct in its claim that, in the single soul, a good "education," comprising music, gymnastics and appropriate stories, can reprogram wanton desires and align conflicting goals to allow a "good" life (*eudaimonia* or human flourishing is the goal of just ordering). However, where the homesite contains more than one being, the likelihood grows ever more slim that even the most skillful management can duplicate these salubrious effects on diverse beings without violating their individual integrities. Unless the goal of "ordered unity" can be made less absolute, violences will invariably need to be called into play to achieve the desired "order" and homogeneity.

Husserl

Plato and Nietzsche have been helpful to the present project because they permit an exposure of the task of home-craft from the lofty positions of the "domineering natures" and the all-knowing "philosopher-kings." Their accounts of ascetic and psychic remodeling of homespaces expose the violences, both external and internal, that inhere in projects of "order." It is curious and significant that both thinkers posit the violences inherent in the task of home-craft as inevitable and "natural" and therefore "just." Whether they mean these characterizations as "honest" descriptions of forces encoded in the cosmos, or whether they intend them as ironical and revelatory of the ambiguities of justice and life must ever remain an enigma to be interpreted according to the individual discretion of those who take up the "bastard sons" of their writings.[6]

This irresolvable paradox notwithstanding, Plato and Nietzsche appear to expose the violences of home-craft with the frank objectivity of a scientific observation.[7] The shift of philosophical perspective known as the phenomenological approach assumes a wholly different attitude toward phenomena so that the view of a thing is no longer considered as a scientific matter of fact, but, elevated in its specific peculiarity, a thing is encountered in the intuitive awareness of its presentive act. In this heightening of peculiarity, things are accepted simply as what they present themselves as being, within the specific limits in which they present themselves in each case. That is to say, simply, that the phenomenologist attempts to describe the "human" experience of a phenomenon in a seeing that is not a judging.

This does not mean to imply that phenomenological "seeing" is judgment- or value-free. The encounter of subject with object is always value-laden, and though, to the subject, things encountered will always appear valuable, useful and pleasurable (in varying degrees), but the subject will interpret these valuations as objectively derived. However, phenomenal "seeings" will never be construed as a pure "objectivity" in the broader gaze of the phenomenologist. This gap between the "seeing" of the subject and the "seeing" of the phenomenologist will demonstrate that *from within* the violences that inhere in the subject's pursuit of its life projects will not be perceived *as such*. The phenomenological position will also permit us to witness how the violent strategies for ordering the self can overflow their existential borders and "rebound" onto neighbouring others, without that aggressive "overflow" being perceived as such from inside the experience of agency.

Edmund Husserl was the first to emphasize the value and necessity of the phenomenological approach to get at the *lived reality* of how human beings function in the world. Husserl insists that phenomena come to appearance as a process of disclosure; Plato and Nietzsche, by contrast, prioritize and present as unproblematic (uncompromised by the object) the conscious creative artistry or "just" psychic ordering of the individual. In his concentration upon the presentive act, Husserl is able to prioritize the *how* of the occurrence of things—the lived experience of their event—over the *what* of the occurrence (scientifically "objective" observation).

By a method of successive "reductions," the phenomenologist achieves a conceptual paring by which he consciously "brackets out" any assumptions beyond the subject's direct intuition of the object of experience. Husserl explains that the phenomenologist "sets aside with full awareness all skepticism together with all 'natural philosophy' and 'theory of knowledge.'"[8] As this bracketing method takes utterly naively each presented thing or event and attempts to bring its peculiarity into view, the phenomenologist brings to observation the human subject and "human" ways that subjects experience particular phenomena.

For Husserl, as for Nietzsche and Plato, subjectivity is a creative act. To be a subject means to be a self-constituting subject, giving meaning and unity to one's experiences. Such constituting, however, for Husserl, is anything but unproblematic, since it involves an inherent paradox (missed by Plato and Nietzsche). The paradox resides in the concomitant facts that the work of the constituting subject is always already complete, even as it remains an ever open task. What this means for a subject is that the "intentionality" through which it fashions the world has always already "found" that world intact, intrinsically meaningful, and value-structured in its primary "originariness." However, the fact of this "originariness" before the event of the subject's "intentionality" does not alter the *lived sense* of world as created by the subject.

The world is for me absolutely nothing else but the world existing for and accepted by me . . . in a conscious *cogito*. It gets its whole sense, universal and specific, and its acceptance as existing, exclusively from such *cogitations*. In these, my whole world-life goes on, including my scientifically inquiring and grounding life. By my living, by my experiencing, thinking, valuing and acting, I can enter no world other than the one that gets its sense and acceptance or status in and from me, myself.[9]

According to Husserl the world appears *as world* and *can* only appear as world. It is always already intelligible as lived. It is true that cracks can occur in that world, ruptures in the schematic framework that contains and shapes phenomena. New facts can confront the subject that threaten the accepted meaning system. But these meaning crises tend only to be temporary. The subject soon acts to make the necessary adjustments to the orienting framework, re-sorting the offending data of experience to neatly fit into given concepts or re-adjusting the concepts to accommodate the new data. Thus the horizons of truth are subtly shifted that life can continue to make sense for the subject and world can continue to be world and not chaos.[10]

We have seen that, for Husserl, home-craft involves a paradox. To be a human being carving out a place in a world means to be a subject caught up in the always already completed quest for a place to self-actualize. This does not reduce the significance of the task, however. The questing is no mere pastime but, for Husserl, the very work of life, the fundamental principle of existence.[11] The identifying markers by which the subject sketches out identity can be territorial, human, linguistic or religious, but the subject will maintain an uncanny capacity to discover and recast markers that are meaningful and orienting, even in the most alienating of circumstances, so fundamental and crucial is meaning, coherence and stable self-definition to the functioning lifeworld of the subject.[12]

Husserl's account of subjectivity exposes the subject's assumption that its action is free. This assumption Husserl demonstrates to be crucial to the human task of constituting identity. Being a subject means establishing and ordering a homespace, choosing a site to be and a stage on which to act in relation to a world. It is the phenomenologist, not the subject, who sees the false consciousness of the subject, given the fact of the "originarily" prior completion of that task. The (false) consciousness of free and spontaneous autonomy under which the subject labours is achieved through a double blindness. It lacks a robust sense of its temporal multi-dimensionality and it lacks a sense of its complex interwovenness in the human world of conflicting agencies. Because the sense of freedom is the essential ingredient in human subjectivity, and because freedom maintains within the absolute hegemony of the "now," subjectivity lacks a full awareness of the restrictions that bear on its autonomy.

Ultimately a subject does come to understand, by analogy with its primary experience of free constitution, the experiences of others in their ordered worlds.[13] Furthermore, whatever the temporal focus of the subject, time ultimately creeps in upon it. The lifeworld is always being infected by other dimensions of time, through the "retention" of the past and the "protention" of the future that steal into present schemata. What is important, however, is that the subject remains largely oblivious to external and multi-dimensional forces because of the paradox that the always already constituted human world is always being lived as a "present" realization, as a *subject's enactment* of truth.

Husserl's discovery of the drastically restricted temporal and inter-subjective awareness of the subject reveals a blindness that is simultaneously an ethical limitation that links to the violences inherent in the task of home-craft.

The subject's fascination with the present renders freedom *as identity*, and that rendering makes of freedom, without apology or remorse, an absolute and supreme value, dedicated to the task that is the fundamental and crucial principle of life. Given the importance of the task, it is difficult to see how any act in its interest, any egoism could be construed by the subject as anything but necessary and inevitable.[14]

Heidegger

The claim of the absolute freedom of the subject and the absence of any sense of historical or inter-subjective complexity within the subject's lifeworld are features of Husserl's phenomenology that compelled Heidegger, like so many of Husserl's students, to remove himself radically from the camp of the master. In Heidegger's work, the removal is achieved by a subtle shift of the phenomenological lens through which the subject's world is encountered. Heidegger problematizes the free spontaneity of the subject by exposing that the subject's ways of being open to a world are always already entangled in a complex web of interactions. This shift highlights the fact that the subject is present and active but also passive and receptive. To put this another way, Heidegger seeks to reinstate the power of the object in the phenomenal relation of subject and object. The world is not only a prior construction intact and positioned as object over against a subject, but it has always already shaped itself around a subject and shapes the subject with its already established "truths," all the while of the subject's experience of unfettered freedom and spontaneity.

Heidegger recognizes that prior, highly complex systems of meaning largely predetermine how the subject's world will be constituted, how he will "find" himself free and functional within that world, and thus how he will understand the extent and nature of the future possibilities open to him. This prior constitution does not negate but complicates the subject's experience of spontaneous freedom. To restate this in Heideggerean terms, *Dasein* is "thrown" into a world of truths and meanings that precede its arrival and, these truths remain mostly unconfrontable, at *Dasein*'s back, so to speak. This is why being-in-the-world is largely a "falling" in Heidegger's account. *Dasein* remains unaware of its historical and inter-subjective indebtedness, submersed in previously constituted value-systems and meaning structures, like a cart-horse with blinders, "tranquilized and 'understanding' everything."[15]

Husserl makes it the task of the philosopher to step outside the subject position, remove the blinders and see the difficulties of immersion within pre-constituted systems of meanings and values. However, Heidegger refuses the possibility of Husserl's "philosophical position." There is no way to achieve the pose of disinterested spectator precisely because we are all equally immersed in a "human" world and have no means of escaping that immersion. To highlight this impossibility, Heidegger speaks of the "mood" of *Dasein*. Mood sets the tone of *Dasein*'s comportment toward the world. Mood is something which is always with *Dasein*, like permanently affixed spectacles with shifting lenses that determine at every moment how *Dasein* will "find" the outside world. Heidegger states:

> The fact that moods can deteriorate and change means simply that in every case Dasein always has some mood. The pallid evenly-balanced lack of mood, which is often persistent and which is not to be mistaken for a bad mood, is far from nothing at all.[16]

Heidegger emphasizes the restrictions rather than the freedom of the subject in three distinct ways: (1) by insisting on the "throwness" of the subject into prior constituted systems of meaning and value, (2) by asserting that the blinders of mood will offer a "primordial disclosure" that will *predetermine* the fundamental modes that being-toward-a-world will assume and (3) by maintaining that this "primordial disclosure" reaches depths far greater than any cognitive act can achieve.[17] These factors ensure that the very phenomena that can arise for a subject, that is, the possibilities for being that might arise for a subject and the possible modes of encounter with those beings, only come to possibility because human beings are never disinterested, any more than they are ahistorical or inter-subjectively free. A subject in a world is always an engrossed and concerned member of that world, immersed within its meanings and its valuations.

Levinas

French Lithuanian philosopher, Emmanuel Levinas, student of Husserl and Heidegger, takes up the limits in "phenomenal seeing" for achieving ethical being, in light of the subject's simultaneous misperceptions of its radical freedom and its absolute innocence. Levinas finds it ethically strategic to begin from Husserl's paradox of subjective experience as unfettered freedom from world and historicity. Levinas posits that, because of the subject's blindness to its immersion in a prior-constituted and "human" world, lived experience is incapable of adequate access to the ethical. The subject cannot see what it receives through its histories or what it owes to environing others, since it is engrossed with the work of its freedom in carving out a world.

Levinas acknowledges the value of the Heideggerean shift of perspective that opens up the historicality of the subject and underscores identity as inter-subjectively woven. Levinas also agrees with Heidegger that the subject is always already an interested and concerned member of its world, submerged within that world's meanings long before any freedom comes into play. But Levinas mourns Heidegger's loss of an accurate sense of the lived experience of subjective life. He is not satisfied with Heidegger's depiction of interested and concerned living as "falling" and inauthentic. For Levinas, living being is peaceful, simple and, above all, sincere. Life is pure enjoyment *even* in the face of death. After all, he argues, "the condemned man still drinks his glass of rum."[18]

Levinas is also unsatisfied that Heidegger fails to make any ethical use of his insight into the subject's historical and inter-subjective indebtedness. Heidegger's concentration upon the multi-dimensionality of the "now" and its pre-grounding in the past misses the one dimension of existence that makes it, in Levinas' estimation, an ethical life. Primordial to the "now" and much more historical than any personal history, Levinas posits an ethical demand encoded as a divine decree, a command from a higher dimension of being that ordains the life of the neighbour the responsibility of the one who finds himself in proximity to the neighbor's need. To have been blessed with life, to realize one's identity as "human," is to respond to this demand, inscribed in the face of the needy other—the widow, the orphan and the alien.

For Levinas, the limits of subjective vision present a problem for ethics and, as ethics is "first philosophy," Heidegger's failure to address these limits *as ethically meaningful* is an unforgivable flaw in his otherwise ingenious work. It is not enough for the philosopher to expose what "is" for subjectivity. What "ought be" is the most essential domain of the philosophical, insists Levinas, especially in a post-Holocaust world. For ethical being, there must exist a subject *free for* action and responsibility, a subject answerable for itself, a subject open to the call of what *must be* beyond what *is*. Levinas explains where Heidegger misses the ethical mark:

> For Heidegger, [though] existence certainly does have a meaning . . . the subject is neither free nor absolute; it is no longer entirely answerable for itself. It is dominated and overwhelmed by history, by its origin, about which it can do nothing, since it is thrown into the world and this abandonment marks all its projects and powers.[19]

Levinas situates himself between the phenomenological positions of Husserl and Heidegger but departs profoundly from both. He attempts to maintain the lived experience of subjective freedom predominant in Husserl's work, while correcting the sense of the comfortable enworldedness of the subject and the absoluteness of its freedom. On the other hand, Levinas refuses the subject the overpowering sense of utter enslavement to history and to the world that he believes makes Heidegger's account "insincere" to the lived experience, and, worse, exaggerates the power of histories to the point where subjects can no longer act freely or responsibly.

Thus, Levinas attempts a re-description of the lived experience of subjective existence that highlights what is *missing* from that experience. Levinas demonstrates how the subject can, in pursuing its "egoisms," violate environing others without the slightest regard for their interests—without "regarding" them *as* having interests—and this permits the subject to maintain an absolute sense of innocence about its violations. Levinas shows that, from the sanctity of the homespace, immersed in the crucial project of its (re)formulations of world, the subject is safely and blindly detached from the ethical, self-concerned and out of touch with the concerns of the surrounding world, secure within its "domicile" and utterly "for itself"—egoist and alone in its "ontological adventure." He states:

> In enjoyment I am absolutely for myself. Egoist without reference to the Other, I am alone without solitude, innocently egoist and alone. Not against the Others, not "as for me . . . but entirely deaf to the Other, outside of all communication and all refusal to communicate—without ears, like a hungry stomach.[20]

Levinas' account of the lived experience of home-craft highlights the ethical inadequacies of the subjective position, but Levinas faithfully maintains the inevitability of the violences visited upon surrounding others. For Levinas as for Nietzsche, living being *is* violating being, appropriating being, consumptive being, Levinas insists over and over.[21] Paradoxically, he also insists repeatedly that the subject acts in purest innocence, outside of all cognition of the needs of environing others—"innocently egoist and alone."

Levinas challenges Husserl's claim that the subject always already finds himself in a world that is fully constituted, meaningful and comfortable. Rather, for Levinas, the subject takes up existence as a task of establishing a safe house within the chaotic and the alien materiality—"the elements"—through action perceived from within as pure spontaneity and freedom. A subject throws itself as an ecstatic self-propulsive project into its existence. The event of human being is, for Levinas, pure work, deed, activity; an individual self-actualizes by "polarization" within "Being-in-general," breaking free from Being's overwhelming grasp by projecting itself into identity. Being, as individual existence, is a struggle for stable self-definition, achieved through a freedom felt as absolute. One must muster "the power to maintain oneself identical above the variations of becoming."[22]

The subject erupts as an individual entity through an act of sheer freedom while "Being in general" all the while threatens, as a hum, as a rustle, as a buzz, as a chaos of meaninglessness, to overwhelm and consume the subject and efface its particular identity. It is not merely fear of death that drives the project of existence (though it is that too) but it is fear of endless, meaningless persistence in alienating, undifferentiated, "suffocating" being that terrorizes the subject and propels it into its task. Levinas describes this double angst:

> Existence of itself harbours something tragic which is not only there because of its finitude [23]

and again:

> Being is essentially alien and strikes against us. We undergo its suffocating embrace like the night. [24]

The subject, an obsessive freedom, struggles frantically to carve out a safe "domicile" within this alienating force by throwing itself into the project of assigning orientational markers, boundaries to fix a home terrain. The subject must *impose* coherence on the chaotic by forging meanings and logical relations— relations to itself on the basis of its enjoyments and its needs. It is no accident that, in Levinas' description, this task sounds like a divine creation. Living being lives its freedom like a god, like a hero, oblivious to the needs of others and the violations that inhere in its relations.

According to Levinas, the subject learns to manipulate and gain control over the world of its immediate immersion by identifying with aspects of that world that, though actually "belonging" to the infinite ungraspableness of their own worlds, "belong" to the subject through the subject's annexation of their "sides" through a "knowing."

> Man has overcome the elements only by surmounting this interiority without issue by the domicile, which confers upon him an extraterritoriality. He gets a foothold in the elemental by a side already appropriated: a field cultivated by me, the sea in which I fish and moor my boats, the forest in which I cut wood; and all these acts, all this labour, refer to the domicile. Man plunges into the elemental from the domicile, the primary appropriation. [25]

These "knowings" permit the subject a stable, fixed existence, even amidst the endless flux of the "elemental." The domicile's walls of assigned meanings shut out the chaos of meaningless existence. This extraterritoriality is, however, only ever a superficial appropriation. Things belong to me, are "known," only by the "sides" by which they present themselves to me: *my* mother, *my* friend, *my* fields, *my* church. The walls of my domicile are a false territoriality, having no "depth." My assumption of their "belonging to me" comprises both a violation of the object's independence and integrity, and a false security for the subject, a mere illusion of fixed stability. Beyond the "sides" of my surrounding others that form the safe walls of my domicile, the things themselves drift endlessly away into the infinity of their own private existences, each of these annexed "sides" themselves opening onto endless worlds carved out of their own meanings in the chaos.

Levinas' description of existence as the construction of a "domicile" through annexation of the "sides" of others may resonate with Heidegger's metaphor of "use" as the human mode of being-in-the-world. But Levinas refuses that the subject merely "uses" others. Relationships with other beings can best be understood, asserts Levinas, on the model of consumption. The distinction between utilization and consumption may not be readily apparent but the structure of these relations is entirely different. While it is true that eating is useful to human beings and can be analyzed as a merely pragmatic necessity, this analysis is scientific and reflective and not at all the *lived* experience of a subject. Eating, in its lived reality, is utterly sincere and innocent, contends Levinas. It is a genuine relationship of enjoyment that is valued for its own sake. In consuming, I make the other me, for the sheer pleasure of an assimilation that overcomes the alienating force of Being. Levinas states:

> To be sure, in the satisfaction of need, the alienness of the world that founds me loses its alterity; in satiety the real I sank my teeth into is assimilated, the forces that were in the other become *my* forces, become me. [26]

What is crucial to an understanding of Levinas' seemingly self-contradictory account of the "ontological adventure" as simultaneously "innocent" and "consumptive" of environing others is fathoming the depth of the menace that structure's the event of existence and fashions "consumption" as so fully pleasurable and "innocently" sincere that it is ethically blind.

Levinas' subject, like that of Husserl's account, remains locked in the endless "now" of its projects, never escaping the angst that drives it obsessively, never evading either death or its alienation from Being, but condemned to an eternity of evasive action in identity work. But, ironically, presence, this condemnation, resonates with the horror of Being. It is suffocating and terrifying. To be, even as freedom, is to "enter into the seriousness of eternity."[27] To exist is to usher in the impossibility of disengaging from existence. Freedom carves out a domicile where its labours keep it occupied to the extent that it can forget the suffocating endlessness of being, but, ironically, even the domicile, with its secure enclosure from the elements, will ultimately prove another site of imprisonment, an "interiority without issue."

The subject escapes that asphyxiating interiority only in moments of pleasure, entirely gripping because entirely sincere. The naïve enjoyment of consumption comprises the way that the subject breaks free of anonymous Being and achieves self-identity, and it is also the way that the subject "knows" and identifies others in acts of representation. Things, people and events take on meanings for a subject precisely because consumption translates the "sides" of things into cognition and discourse. Because consumption can forget the "depth" of things, their fluctuations and their complexity, the subject is able to forge logical relations and assign meanings, and fix them in a language that categorizes differences under common rubrics that efface their infinite mysteriousness.[28] In these ways, the subject can outsmart the capricious world of empirical flow that would otherwise overwhelm it and choke out its identity and its world.

All relations are, for Levinas, violational. Knowing, greeting, enjoying, caressing, welcoming, explaining, loving, apologizing are all violent gestures, all cognitive aggressions that violate the integrity of the other and reduce its wondrousness to the "sameness" of appropriative relation. The violence of these relations is seen by the ethically hyper-sensitive philosopher. He describes the subject:

> for itself as the "stomach that has no ears," capable of killing for a crust of bread . . . for itself. [29]

But, under the phenomenological reduction in the immediacy of the lived experience, what comes to view is only the innocent enjoyment that appreciates, savors and genuinely values—as it consumes—the other. Consumption is entirely innocent, peaceful, simple and sincere. "The man who is eating is the most just of men," Levinas insists.[30] The "for itself" of a subject is a function of a simple misunderstanding. The subject is:

> as the surfeited one who does not understand the starving and approaches him as an alien species, as the philanthropist approaches the destitute.[31]

The innocent subject cannot see the violence that structures its being-in-the-world. It cannot peer into the infinite depths beyond the "sides" of the things it violates. It cannot hear the cries of the hungry that would share its crust of bread. Locked in the deafness and tunnel vision of its consumptive representations, bound within the eternal presence of its anxious enterprise, the subject cannot gain access to the ethical. It cannot escape the domicile to gain the distance of reflection, a distance that might afford it an objectivity and a vision of the needs of others. The subject is condemned to living consumptively without ever knowing how voracious its modes of being.

For Levinas, violence structures the entire event of living. It is "characteristic of the whole of our being-in-the-world."[32] The domicile cleaves an opening for particular identity within the undifferentiated totality of Being, only to itself become a totalizing apparatus that appropriates alien identity and assimilates it to the homesite. However, after demonstrating his subtle appreciation for the violences that characterize life, Levinas makes a compelling phenomenological move. He reclaims consumptive subjectivity, not only as "innocent" and ethically blind, but as utterly necessary and desirable. The "ontological adventure" becomes the existential stage upon which the ethical moment can occur. After all, empty hands cannot feed the hungry; only those who have can give. The injunction from a higher dimension of being to be the brother's keeper occurs in an "anarchic" time long before the "ontological adventure" is begun. But the "ontological adventure" must be accomplished prior to the ethical event because, though man may not live by bread alone, justice begins with bread.

Thus the "ontological adventure" is a most necessary (though not sufficient) condition for ethics. Consumptive, rapacious being is innocent, necessary, inevitable and desirable. Though, for Levinas, freedom ceases to operate in the dimension of the ethical, good works occurring largely "against the will" of the subject of good—through him and despite him, rather than by his willing agency—there is no guarantee that goodness will happen. The only sure thing is the violent project that prepares for its advent.

Philosophical Resonances

Nietzsche's shocking honesty about the violent artistry that powers the (for him) ascetic project of home-craft and describes active, noble, robust being-in-the-world resonates with the elitist dominations of Plato's philosopher-king, Bruce Lincoln's priestly oppressors, and the self-purifying consumptiveness of the self-realizing subject under the phenomenologist's gaze. It makes one wonder whether Socrates meant the naïve declaration that all men love and seek the good as an empirical observation or as yet another of his ironies. Our lived experience is that people often claim to love the good but simply do not seek it in their daily interactions. The good can be tiresome, demanding, and bewildering. The citizenry of Athens once voted into exile a man called Aristeides the Just, not because he had performed any particularly evil deed or posed any real threat to the stability of the polis, but because they simply tired of hearing him referred to by that annoying epithet.[33]

Notes

1. F. Nietzsche. *The Gay Science.* tr. Walter Kaufman. New York: Vintage Books, 1974. Section 290.

2. I suspect, however, that the most domineering natures follow laws that, though *experienced* as entirely "their own," have their origins in the wider network of their relations, fashioned by their particular and their specific histories and ordained by their cultural ancestors and gods. I also suspect that less "strong and domineering natures" may approach the task of identity formation in a similar if less haughty way, self-realizing according to visions of "perfection" and restrained by ascetic "constraints," again not entirely their own but bequeathed by their histories and reinterpreted within the unique web of their interrelations, in response to the distinctive circumstances of their times and places.

3. F. Nietzsche. *On the Genealogy of Morals.* tr. Walter Kaufman. New York: Random House, 1967. 87.

4. At the close of Book IX of the *Republic* (592a ff.), Socrates admits that the "just city" is not likely ever to be realized on earth, but serves as a pattern for ethical conduct for good men seeking justice in their own souls.

5. Bruce Lincoln. *Myth, Cosmos and Society: Indo-European Themes of Creation and Destruction.* (Harvard University Press. 1986). 153. A similar connection with Eastern patterns of social dominance and oppression was the subject of E. J. Urwick's *The Platonic Quest.* (Santa Barbara, California: Concord Grove Press. 1983. first published London: Methuen. 1920). See also Bruce Lincoln. *Death, War and Sacrifice: Studies in Ideology and Practice.* (Chicago: University of Chicago Press. 1991).

6. At *Phaedrus* 278a, Plato has Socrates state that the written word is dangerous because, like a bastard son, it can run all around saying anything to anyone without the guidance of its father.

7. Methods of observation that make claims to objective truth Husserl would equate to a "theoretical" or "scientific" attitude that claims objectivity only by missing the fact that original observations were always direct intuitions of particular objects.

8. Edmund Husserl. *Ideas Pertaining to a Pure Phenomenology and to a Phenomenological Philosophy.* tr. I. F. Kerston. (Dordrecht and Boston: Kluwer Academic Publishers. 1983). 47.

9. Husserl. *Cartesian Meditations.* (Dordrecht: Kluwer Academic Publishers. 1995). I.8. 21.

10. Note the resonance of Husserl's account of lived experience of the confusing data of empirical experience with Walter Burkert's theory of the dual "containers."

11. The fundamental and crucial nature of this task for the subject explains, in the opinion of Husserl's student, Erazim Kohák, the curious tendency of human beings to stay on in their "homelands" long after those homes have become alienating and unfriendly places for them. Kohák states, "Once we have grasped that principle [of the fundamentality of the task of home-craft], we can understand why, for instance humans endure rather than emigrate, or why a human can identify with a group of persons, a language, or a religious faith in place of a territory." *Idea and Experience.* (Chicago: University of Chicago Press. 1978). 81-82.

12. This fact is illustrated, poignantly, in the personal lives of Husserl and his student and fellow phenomenologist, Jan Patočka, both of whom stayed on in their "homelands" long after they had become marginalized and excluded from full participation in the academic life of the group, forbidden to teach or publish.

13. For an interesting complication of Husserl's theory of inter-subjectivity by analogy from the living body, see Johanna Maria Tito. *Logic in the Husserlian Context.* (Evanston, Ill.: Northwestern University Press. 1990). 166-211.

14. The subject cannot see beyond the "now's" of the lived experience, so the recovery of the depth of time, for Husserl, becomes the task of the philosopher. Since, for Husserl, a subject's experience of world is a "human" experience of a "human" world shared by human beings who understand each other, human acts have an analogous structure that not only ensures the possibility of inter-subjective communication but that actually ensures communication as an experiential given long before it becomes a philosophical problem. The philosopher's task is to uncover the "human" ways that world is encountered and to articulate that truth as a universal "human" experience.

15. Martin Heidegger. *Being and Time.* tr. John Macquarrie, Edward Robinson. (San Francisco: Harper-Collins. 1962). I.5B. 38. 222. See also I.5B 210-211.

16. Heidegger. *Being and Time.* I.5A29. 173.

17. Heidegger. *Being and Time.* I.5A29. 173.

18. Levinas. *Existence and existents.* 45.

19. Levinas. *Discovering Existence with Husserl.* (tr. Richard A. Cohen, Michael B. Smith. Evanston, Ill: Northwestern University Press. 1998). 84. Note, in Levinas' description of Heideggerean angst and in his own account of the anxiety of the existent in the face of Being, how the tragic bearing at the root of human existence resonates with the "nostalgia" that I suspect is bequeathed by our myths.

20. Levinas. *Existence and existents.* 134.

21. See especially Levinas' essay "The Ego and the Totality" in *Collected Philosophical Papers* and *Totality and Infinity.* "Enjoyment and Representation."

22. Levinas. "Philosophy and the Idea of Infinity" in *Collected Philosophical Papers.* 47-59. 51.

23. Levinas. *Existence and existents.* 20.
24. Levinas. *Existence and existents.* 23.
25. Levinas. *Totality and Infinity.* 131-132.
26. Levinas. *Totality and Infinity.* 129.
27. Levinas. *Totality and Infinity.* 34.
28. For a full treatment of this subject, see Levinas. *Totality and Infinity.* 139.
29. Levinas. *Existence and existents.* 118.
30. Levinas. *Existence and existents.* 44.
31. Levinas. *Existence and existents.*
32. Levinas. *Existence and existents.* 45.
33. Plutarch. *Lives.* Aristeides. Book 7.1-8.

Chapter 6

The Ambiguities of Home

a phenomenology
of identity-construction

Shortcomings in the Philosophical Accounts of Home-Craft

In the previous chapter, I have presented various philosophical accounts of identity-formation and consolidation. Whether the approach was idealistic, existential or phenomenological, whatever the diverse imagery or philosophical method employed, however unique the angle from which the problem of home-craft was attacked, resonant paradoxes emerged that disclosed tensions between the *lived* experience of free and spontaneous agency as "innocent" and "heroic" and the philosopher's view of the subject's actual effects upon other beings, both within and external to the homespace.

This seemed to be connected in most accounts to the subject's inability to understand its true indebtedness to history and world. Put less abstractly, the philosophers surveyed seem to agree that an individual is so intently focused upon the immediate business of her life that she misses the fact that her view of perfection and her understandings of moral behaviors issue from historically configured understandings of self and world and from the influences of those environing others that compose the "human" world. The clearest resonances among the philosophical accounts of home-craft lay in the recognition of the "egoisms" whereby subjects go about their identity work in the world, egoisms that, no matter how oppressive to others within the homespace or violational of environing others, are *lived* as innocent, necessary and inevitable.

In Levinas' language, the "ontological adventure" is *lived* as "heroic." Heroes may be tragic, implicated in many an impropriety (like Oedipus, who really did kill his father and marry his mother), but they are rarely *knowingly* wrong. They are active and not reactive. They understand themselves to be shaped from within according to personal visions of perfection. Their identities, the unique qualities that make them "heroic" are not understood as issuing from relations with others; "me" is not seen as a function of the "not-me." Though the hero would not be special without the environing human world over against which he distinguishes himself, the hero largely misses the fact that his distinctness *depends* upon his differences *from others*. His exceptionality could not be posited without them. The hero misses how he *actually* fits and functions in a world because he sees himself "elevated" and, at least to some degree, transcendent with regard to the mundane. The hero cannot see how his superiority, emanating from and manifest in his status, authority, and prestige within the community, is meaningless outside of human relations. Psychologist Rollo May explains the infinitely integrated structure of the human world thus:

> Each person exists in an interpersonal web, analogous to magnetic fields of force; and each one propels, repels, connects, identifies with others. Thus such considerations as status, authority, and prestige are central to the problem of power.[1]

The hero misses the complexity of the human world. He misses the fact of his immersion in an intricate social fabric. He misses that his uniqueness is carved out against that complex fabric. It is *what shows up missing* from the view of the hero that permits him his false perception of himself as free from influence by others and "elevated" with regard to them. *What he misses* confirms not only his blindness to influence, but his blindness regarding concerns beyond the borders of his own identity, his freedom from responsibility *to those others* who stand in real and mutual relations with him. It is these factors of reality that, because *showing up missing*, render persuasive the anthropologists' claim that violent dispositions are inscribed so deeply in human ways of engagement that they generally cannot be located and confronted from within the sanctity of the homespace. The subject's tunnel vision also suggests that certain violent practices have become so deeply absorbed into the lifeworld's conceptual parameters that they conform to, and perhaps themselves configure, visions of perfection and ideal behaviors. Thus it becomes difficult, if not impossible for the subject, focused upon the present of its adventures, to confront its ideals as faulty, its behaviors as destructive, its systems and institutions as oppressive and territorially aggressive. It is precisely what *shows up missing* from the view of the subject that becomes our clue that the anthropologists may be correct that our violent histories have predisposed us toward destructive and unjust ways of being-in-the-world.

In the subject's obliviousness to the fact that it is otherness that permits and in fact configures its uniqueness, the subject is reduced to living out its relations with otherness in the morally bankrupt mode of "consumption." Furthermore, blind to the infinite depth of radical alterity beyond the "sides" that are appropriated for self-realization, the subject misses the ontological fact of the other's resistance to its "consumptive" processes. The subject misses the fact that identity work is an illusion. All the while those "consumptive" processes are appropriating things for the purpose of cognition and representation, those things remain infinitely other—things dynamic, things alive, things extending profoundly beyond the shallow possibilities of knowledge.

What the subject misses is that stability within the flux of empirical reality is an utter impossibility, the oppression of irrepressible change a sheer illusion. The vitality and vigour of living being is ever elusive, ever exploding the unifying forces of identification and representation. It is sheer fantasy that configures living beings as enduring essences that function as points of reference to distinguish identity sites. Conceptualization, identification, representation, articulation in language are all self-deceptive maneuvers that permit only a pseudo-disclosive relation with other beings. Ordering mechanisms imposed upon the chaos of existence to organize and subdue the infinite data of experience into meaningful concepts and categories that support self-identity are hoaxes played upon the self, as illusory as the mythical monster-gods that imposed order on the primordial chaos and started the clock on human time. But this fact *shows up missing* from the view of the subject carving out its identity and making sense of its world.

The accounts of identity formation offered by the various philosophers are most helpful in identifying the blind spots in the view of the heroic subject. But there is a curious aspect of home-craft that I believe to be missing from the philosophical accounts that I have rallied in the previous chapter. It seems to me that, if there is any general weakness among the treated accounts, it resides in the claim that a focused clarity is descriptive of the subject's inner vision of its "ontological adventure." I suspect that that description of subjectivity is not true to the actual lived experience of home-craft, but, rather, that subjects often have a robust sense of the ambiguousness of their loyalties and ideals. They often *feel* conflicted, torn between battling allegiances, compelled to incompatible rights and responsibilities at the differing sites and on the multiple levels upon which identity is simultaneously being established. And I imagine that ideals of integrated, unified existence haunt the conflicted subject and, for many, heighten the sense of failure at life's essential task.

In this chapter, then, I shall attempt a fresh phenomenology of home-craft that highlights not the focused clarity of the subject engrossed in identity work, but the ambiguities that inhere in the task itself, ambiguities that, I believe, are apparent *as ambiguities* in the lived experience of home, ambiguities that complicate and frustrate the task of ordering the homespace in the world of environing and conflicting identity systems.

A Phenomenology of Home

The accounts of identity work treated in the previous chapter concentrated upon the work of the subject carving out a secure homespace for itself in the comfortable—or threatening—world. But they ignored the fact that identity work, the art of home-craft, is carried on, at varying degrees of intensity, in simultaneous and conflicting sites of identity and on many different levels. Identity is carved out in the projects of "centered" and "integrated" individuals (gathered about personal goals and visions of perfection) as families and households (gathered about notions of blood relation and genetic coincidences), in racial, tribal and religious power centers (gathered about ideas of illustrious histories, notions of "home-lands" or special relations with the supernatural), at sites of national loyalties and political ideologies (around ideals of justice or goals of global or territorial extension), and, indeed, at the level of the global community (where notions of species identity posit commonalities in human "nature" or in "natural" rights or responsibilities thought to be extensive and binding to the species).

A consideration of the homespace at each of these various sites exposes a remarkable coincidence of structure: the homespace emerges as irresolvably self-conflicted, a living paradox of freedom and repression, a truly Janus-faced reality. This is because of an ambiguity residing in the very essence of the work of the homespace, lodged in deeply internal conflicts that inhere in the nature of the task itself. These conflicts in the mission of the home come to dictate conflicted ethical messages, positing conflicting ideals of behavior. The internal conflicts are expressed in ambiguous modes of comportment practiced toward co-dwellers in the home and toward other proximate beings. It is this internal self-contradiction, I shall claim, that militates against the possibility, or at least the probability, of purely disinterested action in the world, and also against the probability of self-critical honesty with regard to the destructive strategies employed in identity-construction.

Home, in its lived experience, in the very structure of its living reality, manifests the ambiguities that were enacted in the ritual drama and expressed in the mythical worldview. Its oversimplified, starkly polarized, dialectically split configuration issues from the fact of its conflicted mission in the world. But this is because the site of refuge itself manifests the dialogical ontology communicated in ritual and myth. The living world of the homespace is split between the peaceful, secure, unchanging eternality of the gods and the ancestors (in the sovereign domicile that maintains ordered identity) and the troublesome and risky earthly realm that constantly opens to the chaotic. Let us consider this internal paradox.

The home is primarily and fundamentally understood to be a place of refuge from the chaos. A home must offer shelter, safety and security against the unknown beyond its doors. It must protect all who seek its gentle embrace from the tyranny of mortality and the hostility of the elements. Homes serve as a reference point of belonging in an always chaotic and (to some degree) alienating world. Home is a place of origin, a place of destination and, along life's journey, a site of definition toward which we may look with longing, with loathing, with resentment or with gratitude, but always with a sense of "mine."

This is why it is so interesting—and ironic—that the very site that gives definition to human beings itself defies, in its *lived* definition, all logic of identity. The home, as *lived*, violates the very laws upon which identities find their base, the laws by which we distinguish a thing as unique and self-same, *this* and not another—the laws of identity and non-contradiction. The equivocity of home issues from the "definitive" obligation that a home comprise a refuge. It must be sheltering to those within and without, to indwellers and to those seeking refuge at its doors. Welcoming-home is a bilateral movement, something the very walls and furnishings must offer me as their master, something that I in turn must offer to others as hospitality.

However, this bilateral responsibility is problematic in its lived experience. Let us first consider the aspect of home-craft that, seeking connection with the eternal changeless realm of existence, serves the security of those within. To accomplish this, a home must be prepared to shut its doors and bolt its windows. It must close itself off from the alien and withdraw into a safe interiority. Home-craft requires the establishment of borders to distinguish its terrain, to set it off from the alien, and to create patrolable boundaries. It must be wary when strangers come knocking, for gods and monsters can show up on the unsuspecting doorstep. The safe house must practice a more or less fevered *response-ability*, always alert, never sleeping on its watch, if the inmates are to get their rest. The ever-looming threat of the monstrous must never be forgotten.

A homesite perceived from within as secure may require mere markers of identity, border stones to serve simply as meeting spots with neighbor and passer-by. But where homespaces sense themselves threatened, they can become driven by pathologies of defense. Doors must be bolted and windows secured. Differences passing by the portal will signify danger and trigger domestic alarms. Strangers will be interpreted as threatening, monstrous and perilous and demonic. Guards will need to be posted and the inmates, too, kept under close watch in case of treachery.

Psychiatrist Rollo May warns about the dangers that inhere in an obsessive focus upon security. The most responsible masters can become tyrants of their homespaces out of the very concern for the safety of the loved ones.

> An extreme emphasis on individual responsibility can become an egocentric manipulation of others, a compulsion that defeats genuine morality.[2]

A home, at its most responsible, then, may not be able to avoid assuming an organizational structure that is both oppressive and aggressive. And this impossibility of avoidance approaches completeness the more the household senses itself threatened by a menacing and alien world.

Thus, a curious paradox emerges: the absolutely crucial goal of security is self-defeating for the homespace, since oppressive and aggressive structural organization cannot help but negate the home's equally crucial alter-aspect of hospitality. A fortress-prison is not *experienced* as a home. A home is not *felt* hospitable unless its doors and windows open onto the outdoors, unless indwellers can feed freely upon the nourishing elements. A home must look out over the world of its enjoyment, "consume" directly and "sincerely" the voluptuous presence of the real. A home must *have* its neighbors (in all the ambiguous senses of that possessive verb). It must hail them in their proximity, salute them in respect, but also invite them *in* for refreshment and repose. A refuge, by *lived* definition, must open its larders to the hungry, and offer its protective enclosure—its secure changeless eternality, its "gentleness"—to the road-weary and the forlorn, the shabby and the frail. For the home to be truly home-ly it must provide refuge to the home-*less*. It must put aside its war mask, show a face of welcome and extend a helping hand to the world outside its doors.

Home-craft can take on many forms in the vast array of unique worlds of lived experience. However, its fundamental mission will be one of refuge, maintaining secure stability of definition over against the perilous external chaotic. However, to maintain attentiveness to *both* aspects of this fundamental duty, to fulfill simultaneously the *double* mission implied in refuge, means simultaneously closing the homespace upon the stable eternal abode and opening it to the earthly chaotic that must sacrifice its stable sameness. At every given moment in the performance of the double task, the home will attempt to offer all—internal and external—the safety of the eternal and godlike. However, this being impossible to achieve simultaneously, the home must, at each new moment, situate its urgencies at one of the two extremes of its contradictory task, alternately concentrating on its work as a welcoming refuge for neighbors and passers-by, then abandoning its duty to the external and closing up as a fortress-prison, secured against the confusion of earthly life.

It is the paradox of home that its essence is irresolvably conflicted, and must remain ever conflicted to fulfill its double mission as a refuge. It must remain a *living* paradox, a Janus-faced reality that both nurtures and oppresses its inmates, that offers to the world a visage of both menace and welcome. It must be prepared for the arrival of monsters and gods, and thus must itself play those dual roles, serving as a divine host to its inmates, to its neighbors and needy wayfarers, as a monster menacing its enemies. It must, like the "watchdog guardian" of Plato's "just city," do good to friends and harm to enemies.

These dual roles call for dual sets of virtues, themselves irresolvably conflicted. The fortress-prison must practice warrior virtues, elevating courage, forbearance and loyalty above all other ideal features of character. The special orientation of the fortress-prison (feeling threatened and powerless in confrontation with an alien world and suspicious of those passing by its doors) is inherently unhealthy, say the social scientists. It can incite pathological responses. It is un-*reason*-able to feel constantly under siege and surveillance by others, dangerous to feel debased and dispossessed of power in regard to difference. When homes feel vulnerable, paranoia is not far off, and "pathologies of defense" can abound. "Reasons" for violence can be readily marshaled, as sociologist Neil Smelser explains:

> It is one of the most profound aspects of evil that he who does the evil is typically convinced that evil is about to be done to him. He regards the world or at least a part of it as dangerous or bent on destruction and therefore something justifiably to be destroyed.[3]

A special cognitive framework is erected in the face of the alien when one feels threatened or disempowered. Through this framework the different comes to be viewed as demonic, exaggerated in potency and malevolence beyond all reality. A distorting cognitive framework can develop in whole cultures into an embracing ideology and may even become institutionalized. In individuals and in cultural groups, distorting cognitive frameworks breed pathological responses that readily sanctify violences against alien others. Moreover, the violence in turn sanctifies the hero who annihilates the demon. Heroic "murder" (and the metaphorical murders of torture, expulsion and other brutalities) propagates in the "murderer" myths of moral inviolability and innocence, as well as a conviction of supermundane power. These myths render a false consciousness that grants license to further violence. Such myths propel people to the threshold of violence, sociologists contend.[4]

On the other hand, the driving virtues of the welcoming aspect of the mission, ostensibly salubrious and appropriate for dwelling in a world of infinite differences, can be dangerous to the practitioner and his wards. It is easy to see how the practice of virtues as gentleness, generosity and compassion could only ever be temporary and provisional. The orientation of openness would constantly throw the homesite into risk and inevitably cause it to "rebound" to its "monstrous" warrior aspect. Welcome ultimately fulfills itself in an obsessive militarism that would, ironically, defeat the mission of welcome altogether.

Far more ambiguous, however, is the danger pointed out by social scientists like Viola Bernard, Perry Ottenberg and Fritz Redl. They warn that face-to-face confrontation with a suffering world is dangerous to the onlooker's sense of compassion, placing in jeopardy her very humanity. In their article in *Sanctions For Evil* entitled "Dehumanization," these experts report a phenomenon that affects those who witness first-hand the extreme afflictions of others. They tell that witnesses soon become hardened to the sight of suffering and lose their ability to empathize with the afflicted.[5] It becomes increasingly common and unproblematic to deem the suffering as "less human." Thus witnesses to affliction can themselves become "less human" by virtue of the loss of the human quality of emotional responsiveness. The sociologists call this *bidirectional* hardening "dehumanization" and report that this phenomenon turns caring witnesses into desensitized, apathetic robots. Such hardening is not only undesirable in itself but can burgeon into aggressive overflow. The social scientists report:

the constructive self-protection [that dehumanization] achieves will cross the
ever-shifting boundaries of adaptiveness and become destructive, to others as
well as the self.[6]

It seems, then, that, whether the homespace presents its menacing face or opens
hospitably toward the world, either mission inevitably fulfills itself in an aggressiveness that is destructive, both within the homesite and with regard to its
neighbors.

A further difficulty issues from the fact of the conflicted virtues at the
homesite. The conflict composes an ethical split that results in a moral confusion
that social scientists tell us defeats all moral sense. The dangers of an ethically
ambiguous environment cannot be overstated. "Explosions of passion" often
follow directly in the wake of ethical confusion. When the morally confused
find themselves confronted by an incomprehensible set of circumstances, violence often flares to the surface to impose order on the confusing data. But,
worse, psychologists report that, ultimately, the object-relation disintegrates and
any object will do.[7] René Girard makes a resonant observation:

> Violence is not to be denied, but it can be diverted to another object, [anything]
> it can sink its teeth into.[8]

The disintegration of the object-relation in violent outbursts (in Bloch's
language, "rebounding violence," and on Lorenz's terms, "redirected aggression") may result from the physiological fact that the urge to violence incites
certain physiological changes that prepare people's (especially men's) bodies for
battle. It is far more difficult to quell these impulses, once incited, than to rouse
them in the first place. Again, violent acts are accompanied by great bursts of
energy and that energy often convinces the subject that he has superhuman abili-
ties or license from a transcendent power.[9] A sense of transcendence or transcendent authorization legitimates and impels further violence, while furnishing
a sense of inviolability and a superior vantage point from which to posit "reasons" to prolong and escalate violence. It is dangerous to feel "elevated" with
regard to one's fellows and strangers. It is dangerous to think the gods on one's
side. Yet it seems that it is equally dangerous to feel disempowered, threatened
and helpless with regard to others.

Identity structures, by necessity, must find ways to stabilize their territories.
They must resist the ebbing, flowing, passing-away aspect of their own coming-
to-be. Yet, clearly, they must also resist their own tendencies toward pathological enclosure that will suffocate the indwellers and defeat the lived experience of
the home as gentle and hospitable. They must also resist foolhardy generosity
because the excesses of the world outside its doors constantly threaten self-
identity and security. Being-in-the-world must remain a tireless amoral "consumption" of otherness if the homespace itself is not to be consumed into the
menacing chaos of the elements at large. Home-craft must resist, yet simultaneously maintain, its conflicting yet necessary aspects if it is to endure as an entity.

Nevertheless, no matter how the homespace might attempt to maintain an ethically viable mode of dwelling in the world, every view it has of the world (from the fortress-prison or the welcoming refuge) is likely ultimately to propel it into risk, and then into violent pathologies.[10]

The dialectic of the withdrawal into safe, if suffocating and "representationally" distorting, interiority and the opening to otherness that ushers in renewed fragility and powerlessness—and ultimately psychological and moral collapse—issues, in human relations within the home and with neighboring homes and strangers, not only in patterns of welcome and nurturance, but as recurrent cycles of violence that throw the home into a logic of hyper-responsibility, and eventually into an obsessive self-assertion. In whatever mode the home is currently functional—whether its self-protective warrior virtues are alert at their post or whether doors are thrown open in joyful consumption of the world—it is likely ultimately to erect a cognitive framework that configures as threatening and demonic differences within the structure as well as neighbors and strangers external to it. Whatever aspect of its mission the home is currently serving, it is likely to ultimately flare into violent patterns of behavior, oppressing those within the system and rebounding upon those without.

Notes

1. Rollo May. *Power and Innocence: A Search for the Sources of Violence.* (New York: Norton and Co., 1972). 100.

2. R. May. *Power and Innocence.* 168.

3. Smelser. "Some Determinants of Destructive Behavior" in R.G. Hamerton-Kelly, ed. *Sanctions For Evil.* 15-24. 17.

4. Neil Smelser states: "Myths of innocence enjoy a more or less universal and permanent existence [though they] tend to be activated only under certain historical conditions." ("Some Determinants of Destructive Behavior." 15-24. 20).

5. Research psychiatrist, Robert J. Lifton, has written about the reactions of Hiroshima survivors to the mass deaths and devastation of the bombings. At first, Lifton reports, the witnesses were overcome by the utter horror of the carnage—the dreadful burns and disfigurements, the carcasses strewn about, torn in pieces and stripped of skin. Witness could find no words to express their initial reactions. However, in a remarkably short while, tells Lifton, a common reaction was reported. "Each described how, before long, the horror would almost disappear. One would see terrible sights of human beings in extreme agony and yet feel nothing." ("Psychological Effects of the Atomic Bomb in Hiroshima: The Theme of Death" in *Daedalus, Journal of the American Academy of the Arts and Sciences.* 1963. 462-497. 92).

6. Viola Bernard, Perry Ottenberg and Fritz Redl. "Dehumanization" in *Sanctions For Evil.* 102-124. 107.

7. See May. *Power and Innocence.* Chapter 9. "The Anatomy of Violence."

8. Girard. "Sacrifice as Sacral Violence" in *The Girard Reader*. James G. Williams, ed. New York: Crossroads Publishing, 1996. 74.

9. Neil Smelser voices this tendency in "Some Determinants of Destructive Behavior" in *Sanctions For Evil*. 15-24. This fact resonates curiously with the elevated and transcendent sense of themselves achieved by Bloch's Orokaiva warrior-hunters as they slaughter their pig "brothers." See *Prey into Hunter*.

10. Walter B. Cannon, in his celebrated work, *The Wisdom of the Body*, tells that there are three possible reactions to situations of threat: flight, fight or delayed response. We may attack in an immediate and cathartic explosion of violence, we may run away and hide, or we may bide our time for a more thoughtful, perhaps more subtle, violence in a future opportunity. (New York: Peter Smith Pub., 1978). Rollo May has shown that those who run away and hide *are* those who wait, and he claims that this group is the most dangerous of all. What they await is sometimes a titanic explosion of destructiveness. (*Power and Innocence*. Introduction).

Chapter 7

Violence *as* Community

the suffocating embrace of the home

In the preceding chapters I have attempted to track into the homespace evidence that the violent mechanisms bequeathed by ritual histories are still at work in modes of identity formation and consolidation as they are carried out in the lived experience of human beings in the modern world. I have noted that, on many levels of identity, conflicts within the task and between conflicting aspects of the task configure home-craft a living paradox, conflicted in its very essence. It is clear that, whatever the benign intentions of the homespace with regard to its inmates, its neighbors and needy strangers, warrior virtues will ultimately take charge of the site and order its conflicted aspects in the interest of security. It is also clear that the more seriously responsible the master of the domain, the more threatening the different may appear, and the more obsessively might he impose ordering strategies to keep out "contaminating" elements and maintain order and homogeneity within the site. Given the essential and inevitable discordance of all homespaces (precisely because composed of diverse elements), it is ironic and yet understandable, that such enormous import is placed upon the achievement of integrity and order within homespaces.

We have seen, in chapter 5, how philosophers understand the task of ordering and integration of homespaces and I have, in the previous chapter, added to their insights my own. In this section, I shall consider familial identity structures, seeking danger signs and potential triggers that might evoke pathologies of defense, ideologies of conquest or consumption, myths of purity, innocence or "elevation," and the overblown mechanisms of order that are prone to legitimate violence.

One inevitable yield of our passion for ordered systems is our passion to give order to worlds beyond our immediate selves. In the words of Martha

Nussbaum, "What does not reach out to order the world does not love."[1] We reach out to the world by trying to understand it. We create harmonious ordered worlds from the confusing flux of existence by ranking and ordering their phenomenal populations according to duly appointed meanings, roles, and functions. All higher vertebrates, Lorenz has told us, advance by developing ranking and ordering systems. One inescapable byproduct of the differentiation that makes possible ranking and ordering is social awareness, self-consciousness about the processes that configure social life.

In ordered systems of social identity, differentiations inevitably result in inequalities. There will be special privileges, special incentives to conform to the ruling logic of the system, specialized forms of coercion to persuade the delinquent parts, special punitive sanctions for those who remain unpersuaded. There will be specialized minions to oversee the ordering processes, to monitor the functioning of the separate parts so that they work for the good of the whole. There will be special social rituals to promote appropriate social composure— prescriptions that align individual parts to the overall goals of the system and prohibitions that deter differences to minimize internal conflict. Myths will take shape that trace out the cosmic margins of identity, circumscribe the ideals of the order and assign its appropriate gods to oversee the venture. Myths will identify sacred objects and define necessary symbols and concepts to keep in place the appropriate worldview.

These features and forces are peculiar to almost all ranking systems in the human world. Ordering strategies of their own accord tend toward obsessive self-reinforcement through the proliferation of social/legal/political rituals: forms filled out in triplicate, licenses to dwell and possess, passports to monitor movement, "intelligence" aids to scrutinize social interactions and locate treachery, consensus reports to define the nature and distribution of local populations, agents to anticipate external dangers to the system and formulate self-justifying propaganda, to reinterpret their defensive pathologies in purified justifications. There will be specialists who define the demonic external and render declarations of war. These persistent, obsessively conservative rituals combine to compose a society in which men, women, and their offspring are increasingly committed to the norms of a system that reflect the ideals, fears, aspirations and goals of nobody in particular, yet (in theory) of everyone in general. They reflect the ideological forces of the system, the *system's* vision of the "good of the whole," while yet indicating the explicit desires and beliefs of no particular member of the social whole, not even its power nodes.

Once the system takes shape, its conservation becomes the focus of all its energies, and the rituals of identity work struggle to accomplish the desired longevity. Identity requires ordering and ordering necessarily involves inequalities—subordinations and elevations, oppressions and oppressors. In the individual soul, this violence may require only the imposition of self-discipline, a violence that suppresses its own wantonness and tempers its own excesses, as reason takes the upper hand and reigns in the horses of passion and appetite so that the "good life" can proceed without internal conflict. Home-craft in the individ-

ual need not be, though it certainly can be (as Nietzsche has intimated) pathological. However, as the project of order reaches out beyond the individual into
communal life—the moment it attempts to embrace more than the solitary
"soul"—there is the rapidly escalating risk that identity strategies will harden
into obsessive and repressive forces that suffocate other beings within the home
and menace those without.

The family unit is the first community of self-definition concentric to the
individual person. It is my contention that tyranny is most easily accomplished
in smaller communities like the marriage or modern "nuclear" family. Sadly, in
many areas of the world including the "enlightened" West, many households are
little better than localized, culturally-legitimated constructs of legalized oppression where rape, prostitution and mental and physical abuse are daily normalities
of the system. The figures recording the incidence of violence in the family
home are astounding. It is equally frightening that violence "rebounds" so effectively between members of the family and from generation to generation across
families. Violence, it as a matter of social scientific record, is very much a "family" affair. Therefore it behooves our project here to determine what features of
the home dispose it toward those violences and whether those features resonate
with the mechanisms of violence identified as bequeathed by ritual histories.

As an identity unit, a household can be defined as an integrated economic,
political and social institution. However, the *lived* definition of household is
something very different from this analytic definition, something much more
intimate with much more than order felt to be at stake. It is *felt* that a family
home is the site of most intimate belonging where members draw together in
closeness and confidence, according to the dictates of nature, to love, nurture,
protect and support one another.

Thus, for many psychologists and sociologists, the principal theoretical
question in understanding domestic violence is how to explain that it is even
thinkable that violence can occur at all in that particular setting. As a matter of
fact, however, there are aspects of family functioning that actually promote violence in the home and encourage the deployment of force and coercion by its
members. When we add these factors to cultural values and beliefs that permit
and indeed institutionalize violent behaviors, we find many "reasons" to explain
why domestic violence is as prevalent as it is in almost all societies.

Violence, in human relations in general and in family relations in particular,
is rooted in the fact of institutionalization, in its structure as a functioning system. We have seen that inequalities in systems are necessary to permit the ranking that serves goals of integrity and order. Inequalities in status, rights and
powers are experienced as desirable because they effect individual identity and
give a sense of meaningful existence. However, in ordered systems, *institutionalized* inequalities rarely issue in the justice of *self*-definition. They generally
tend to repress the development of individual persons by assigning social definitions that confine the person to a given rank and role. Institutionalized inequalities elicit violent reactions from those individuals and groups oppressed within
the unit, as much as from those at the summit of the social ladder.

Families, as much as states or ethnic structures, are built upon inequalities that elevate some of its members and repress others. These inequalities elicit feelings of impotence and frustration precisely where nurturance and intimacy are promised and most expected. The master in charge of the dwelling need not be demonstrably tyrannical for these frustrations to be felt by those under his wing and under his controlling power. Simone Weil has written poignantly of the effect that all human beings, however benign, exert upon one another by virtue of their sheer proximity. She asserts:

> The human beings around us exert just by their presence a power which belongs uniquely to themselves to stop, to diminish, or modify any movement which our bodies design. A person who crosses our path does not turn aside our steps in the same manner as a street sign, no one stands up or moves about, or sits down in quite the same fashion when he is alone in a room as when he has a visitor. [2]

The most benign freedom limits other freedoms about him, exerting an inevitable weight upon proximate others. But where the freedom in question is less than benign, the weight upon proximate others can be crushing. Weil describes how severe situations of coercion transform victims substantially:

> These are not men living harder lives than others, not placed lower socially than others, these are another species, a compromise between a man and a corpse. That a human being should be a thing is, from the point of view of logic, a contradiction. But when the impossible has become a reality, a contradiction is as a rent in the soul. That thing aspires at every moment to become a man and never at any moment succeeds. [3]

Weil's hyperbolic description of the influence a greater power has upon a lesser is shocking, and yet it is not complete. The disempowered are not simply pathetic. Nor are they merely apathetic and "corpse-like." They are dangerous. Sociologists tell us that it is precisely the disempowered who are the time-bombs of a society, ticking away in their frustration to a final and violent explosion.

Yet, revenge is often impossible within the confining walls of the family dwelling. In the worst families, victims have little opportunity to express their frustrations, let alone the energies to explode. The most common victims of domestic violence are women and children because their powerlessness in the family unit is often complemented by their powerlessness in the social structure at large. And the powerless cannot fight or flee their abusers, wherever they find themselves cornered.

Violence is a frightfully frequent visitor to the family dwelling. According to the U.S. Department of Justice Bureau of Justice Statistics, "Violence Against Women: A National Crime Victimization Survey Report" (January 1994), more than two-thirds of violent crimes against women are committed by someone known to them, 28 percent by intimates such as husbands or boyfriends and 5 percent by other relatives. Women may walk city streets at nights with fear, feeling vulnerable to attack, but the reality is that a woman is far more vulnerable to attack by intimates than by strangers. Furthermore, a woman is six times likelier to keep secret her brutalizations by intimates, fearing further reprisals from that loved one. She can try to escape but the further disturbing fact is that brutalizations may not only continue but may increase in frequency and intensity after separation (75 percent of visits to emergency rooms by battered women occur after separation from batterers). It is estimated that a fourth of workplace problems (absenteeism, low productivity, staff turnover, and excessive use of medical benefits) results from family violence. Violence is the reason given for divorce in 22 percent of middle class marriages.[4]

Mary Lystad, in her introduction to *Violence in the Home*, reports that wife battering is often accompanied by sexual and physical abuse of children. Lystad reports that, in a shocking number of modern families, members are subjected to spanking, kicks, bites or punches, and some members are beaten regularly.[5] Sibling violence occurs in a majority of homes. Violence toward the elderly is on the increase. Sexual abuse, like violent physical battering, happens most often within the family home and victimizes both boys and girls. Violence occurs in over half of all American homes, states Lystad, and is documented with comparable frequency and brutality across all social classes and ethnic and racial groups. Twenty to fifty percent of all murders in America, she reports, occur within the family.

How is it that violence is such a frequent visitor to the family home? Lystad explains that family violence has been a problem as long as there have been families. The actual severity of the problem only lately emerged into view. Only in 1962 did battered children syndrome come to public attention. Then, not till the 1970s, did concern expand to embrace battered wives. Elder abuse came to light only very recently, along with premarital and date violence. Yet, centuries ago, John Stuart Mill pointed toward the problem in his essay "On the Subjection of Women":

> However brutal a tyrant she may be chained to—though she may know that he hates her, though it may be his daily pleasure to torture her, and though she may feel it impossible not to loathe him—he can claim from her and enforce the lowest degradation of a human being, that of being made the instrument of an animal function contrary to her inclinations... When we consider how vast is the number of men, in any great country, who are little more than brutes, and that this never prevents them from being able, through the laws of marriage, to obtain a victim, the breadth and depth of human misery caused in this shape alone by the abuse of the institution swells to something appalling.[6]

Mill illuminates the most common form that violence assumes in the sanctity of the family dwelling. It is true that males, far more often than females, are the physical and sexual abusers in the family. Only 5 percent of attacks suffered by men occur at the hands of their intimates. And a woman is six times likelier than a man to keep secret her brutalizations by intimates, because she is much more likely to suffer reprisals from identifying the loved one as her abuser. Annually, compared to males, women suffer ten times as many incidents of violence at the hands of their intimates.

However, men do not hold a monopoly on what Mill has termed brutishness.[7] There are many and varied forms of abuse levied in the "safe enclosure" of the familial sanctuary, out of sight and earshot of neighbors and authorities. Non-physical, psychological aggressions are the weapons favoured by women and children, and these, to be sure, can be even more deeply wounding than beatings. It is not gender, but feelings of power and license, that seems to draw forth aggressiveness. As I have indicated, the ones most vulnerable to violence in the home are generally the least powerful in the family and the society.[8] Powerlessness is no mere coincidence to the fact of victimization, as May has argued persuasively in his *Power and Innocence.* In the past, the penury of economic or political resources to support victims discouraged them from attempting to escape from their situations, so victims rarely voiced their abuses. When victims did manage to escape situations of abuse, they often found themselves with few options but to return to the abusive relationships and face escalated violences. There are a meager 1,500 shelters for battered women in the United States. Yet there are 3,800 animal shelters!

Domestic violence is a logical and predictable consequence of the inequalities inherent in families as ordered ranking systems. It is entirely consistent with the problem at large in society and the world. Institutionalized inequalities (political, economic and social) intrinsic to all systems cultivate feelings of frustration and impotence at every level of social functioning, eliciting violent reactions from oppressed individuals and groups as much as from those in power. The more powerful release their frustrations on the less powerful, and so on down the social scale. It seems that ordered systems operate on, and communicate, the implicit "truth" that any amount of power, however limited, comprises license to violate others less powerful. Only lately have social scientists fully appreciated the fact that violence is viewed as a right.

> Traditional superordinate-subordinate relationships of men and women, adults and children . . . allow for and condone the use of power by those of superior status.[9]

Loving husbands and loving parents, like Nietzsche's creative artists, may be so fixated upon the project of "imposing forms" that they see their violences as necessary tools to be deployed in the name of caring and nurturance. Perhaps it is the very love that binds the household as an intimate society that is the greatest frustrator of peaceful and benign relations. Levinas lists love as one of the tyrant's most effective tools, alongside wealth, torture, hunger, silence and rhetoric.[10] In the worst cases, violence and intimacy become fused in the minds of the victims, since the propaganda and tortures are administered by way of the same body that receives the nourishment and the loving caress. Ideologies that are administered bodily, as we have seen in the case of ancient rituals, are overwhelmingly successful at convincing the victim of the rightness of the status quo of power, sometimes even soliciting the willing consent of sub-groups to their sub-human status and treatment.[11] Fleshy and bloody arguments are deeply and powerfully persuasive and teach the appropriateness of violence across the spectrum of social control.

The least powerful are generally the ones most vulnerable to abuse, and thus, traditionally, women and children have composed the most victimized members of the household. However, the structure of Western homes is rapidly changing and we must be prepared to adjust our attitudes and sensibilities to fit the changing facts. Many women have succeeded in the workplace to the extent that, now, in many households, it is they who compose the economic and social power of the structure. In many modern Western homes, it is the women who rule the family roost. The methods employed to achieve order in the household will vary less with gender than with the ruling power's view of the nature of the project, the degree of urgency attributed to that responsibility, and the "tools of tyranny" at her disposal.

Moreover, socio-cultural factors often offer justification for domestic abuse. Western society, for example, places high value in self-reliance, in the family as elsewhere. This in turn places high value on mechanisms of control. Ironic as it may be, in our "enlightened" Western world, men and women who physically discipline their children are usually deemed by their peers as better parents. Many parents in Western society also promote unconditional respect for those in authority, training their children to do as they are told without asking annoying questions. Unqualified valuations of authority in turn convince both the powerless and the powerful that it is appropriate to use force if necessary to maintain order.

Part of the reason for domestic violences resides in the fact of this small unit's more effective closure. Closure favours the maintenance of myths that legitimate and re-incite the violences. Social myths maintain the institution of marriage sacrosanct however abusive. More localized myths are hard at work as well within the violent household, holding the abusive relationship together in what sociologists name "attribution theories." Batterers tend to attribute their violences to uncontrollable events or to power in others, rather than to any dysfunction in themselves or in the system. There is also the tendency for batterers to blame their victims for their own abuse, a myth all too commonly shared by the victims themselves, explaining why so much abuse goes unreported. Indeed, say the experts, the abused often do contribute to their own abuse. The very strategies they adopt to try to de-escalate the violence can trigger abuse: showing fear and ready submission to unreasonable demands, accepting their abuser's myths of innocence, and mistrusting their own sense of reality.[12] A victim soon assimilates the myths of her abuser as a matter of mental/emotional survival, for her physical safety, and often out of fear for others within the family who are weaker than herself, the old and the children. The worst abusers are known to subject their victims to detailed descriptions of the tortures her loved ones will be made to endure should she tell, leave or seek help outside the household.

As I have indicated, a great part of the reason why the twisted mythologies that justify domestic violences are so persistently successful in dysfunctional households, often shared by abuser and abused alike and even repeating themselves across generations, resides in the fact of the household's very structure.[13] Ironically, the very features of the home that make for warm, intimate mutually-supportive relations simultaneously make it the likeliest site for the eruption and escalation of violence. The home, as intimate, private, "enclosed" space, encourages abuse by the power-seeking members of the family.

Richard E. Gelles lists eleven features of the home that poise it for violence and these bear mention here. First, a great amount of family time is spent in absorbed, intense interaction, far more than the ratio of time spent interacting with others outside the home. This makes the home a place of increased risk for violent outbursts. Secondly, family life embraces a wide spectrum of activities so there are more varied opportunities for conflict. Third, there is a high intensity of involvement within families. Family interactions exact more of an emotional investment than other kinds of encounters. Fourth, family activities are what Gelles calls "impinging activities" that are inherently conflict-structured. The smallest of decisions (what to watch on television, what to eat for dinner, when to go to bed) can structure the terrain of family interaction so that there are always definitive winners and losers.

Fifth, there is an assumed right, within families, to interfere in the affairs of other family members. Sharing a home and mutual caring is often taken as license to influence the values, attitudes, interests, and behaviors of other members of the group. Sixth, age and sex differences within the household widen the potential for conflict across generations and genders. Seventh, the family is one of the few remaining institutions in the modern world that still assigns roles and responsibilities on the basis of age and sex rather than interest or competence. Gelles' eighth feature of the home situating it for violence is one I have previously highlighted—the fact of the household's easy closure. Isolation is a feature sought after by families to amplify intimacy. The family is a private institution that seeks, and generally achieves, insulation from the wider social web. This means that the family is often effectively cut off from the community's protective authorities and from the persuasive effect of public censure.

This fact links to the ninth feature of family life that renders it violence-prone. Families are closed social groups, exclusive organizations. Membership is involuntary and interminable, and involves personal, social, material and legal commitments as well as entrapments. When conflicts arise, giving up one's membership is not so easy as resigning from a voluntary social group. Fleeing the scene of family conflict may offer freedom from beatings and other abuses, but it does not free the victim from a sense of guilt for desertion of her family responsibilities, or from the fear and guilt of having abandoned other family members to the abuses she had been suffering.

The tenth feature is the factor of stress, especially intense in modern Western homes. Change is inevitable within families (births, deaths, adolescence, aging, job loss or promotion, retirement, illness, bad grades), and transitions present ever new challenges and frustrations. Stresses are easily transferred between members in the closed space of the family dwelling. The eleventh feature of the home that Gelles thinks makes it violence-prone is the discomfiting exposure that members suffer when others necessarily share an extensive knowledge of their personal and social biographies. Intimacy and profundity of emotional connection does not permit the personal privacy that makes for healthy individuality. When a whole group knows one's vulnerabilities, likes and dislikes, loves and fears, failings and triumphs, one may feels her deepest secrets nakedly paraded before the group. Such intimate knowledge ought to form the basis for supportive co-dwelling, but it can also be deployed to deeply wound intimates.

Thus, the very structure of the home that poises it for mutual nurturance and support opens it to violence at the hands of its power-seeking members. However, internal factors are not the only dangerous influence upon the family. Part of the reason for domestic violences resides in the fact that society alone decides what constitutes "violence." Social norms are constantly under construction, negotiating the limits between legitimate and illegitimate force, continuously creating new frustrations and pressures that drive individuals to test those limits. Definitions of violence within cultures are regularly re-determined according to current shared meanings and normative understandings, and against the backdrop of inherited axiological valuations fixed into the parameters of the lifeworld. Experts say that society at large, like individual abusers, readily construct myths that shift the blame for family violence to factors and forces outside the family. However, sociologist William Stacey reminds us emphatically:

> Social forces do not batter women and children; conscious, free, responsible men do. They know what they do and research shows they can learn and choose not to batter.[14]

Experts agree that family violence is generated by those who do it simply because they know they can and they know their victims to be powerless to stop them. Like Bloch's Orokaiva pig hunters, violent overflow tends to take the most aggressive form of which the dominant feel themselves capable.

Stacey refuses uncompromisingly to excuse domestic violence as a function of the external features of the society. However, it cannot be denied that modern life in the West causes enormous stresses upon the family. For many, daily life involves the frustration of fundamental human needs. The increased grouping of human activities into large scale organizations makes life for individuals more formalized, more routinized, less "human." When Westerners come home at night to relax before their televisions, the nightly news and the entertainments they view are overwhelmingly violent. Witnessing violence desensitizes us all, to varying degrees, but it is the children who are at greatest risk. Children who are permitted to watch television uncensored are likely to view an enormous amount of violence. We know that children who witness violence—whether in real attacks on self or another family member or in the fictions of television, whether administered to persons or pets or inanimate objects—become less and less scandalized by violence. They become less likely to think violent behavior inappropriate and slower to call for the intervention of adults when they witness incidents of violence.

In the past the frustrations of institutionalized life were satisfied, to some extent, by the knowledge that legalized authorities were sanctioned to return violences upon the offenders. Where trust in the system's legitimated mechanisms of violence remains intact, the general hunger to revenge frustration is gratified vicariously, as René Girard has brilliantly exposed.[15] However, the individual's trust in the legal system to avenge the injustices within the system, and her trust in the power of her own political voice to make necessary alterations in the system has slowly but generally collapsed. There no longer exist effective public outlets for frustration. Perhaps this is why violence has flared to all-time highs in the Western world of late. The greatest evidence of the general belief in the normalcy and acceptability of violence resides in the Western glamorization of violence in its history and its heroes, in its ideals of freedom and individualism, and in the ruling "achievement ethic" that emphasizes winning over the ways that games are played, whether the "game" be little league or big business. The demand for success in competitive systems justifies violent behaviors; it impels those who wish to excel in the rat race toward aggressive and authoritarian tactics.

If the function of intimate societies—marriages and families—is to love and nurture, support and protect one another, as it is *intuitively felt* to be, then the violence that characterizes all too many Western homes is incompatible with their function. We like to think that such things are anomalies—utter absurdities. But, sadly, family violence is not absurd at all but all too intelligible. The project of order, advancing fervently according to Western values of efficiency and effectiveness, most logically dictates that the most responsible household leaders pursue their mission obsessively, even to the point of destructive strategies levied upon beloved family members. The home's promise of gentleness can easily be betrayed, the happiness of individuals can easily be forgotten, in bending the structure toward the goals of order and integrity.

Notes

1. Martha Nussbaum. *The Fragility of Goodness*. Cambridge, Mass.: Cambridge University Press, 1986. 199.

2. Simone Weil. *Intimations of Christianity Among the Ancient Greeks*. Elizabeth Chase Geissbuhler, ed. and tr. London: Routledge and Kegan Paul, 1976. 24-55. 28.

3. Weil. *Intimations*. 28.

4. Most of these statistics have been supplied by National Clearinghouse for the Defense of Battered Women, Philadelphia.

5. Mary Lystad. *Violence in the Home: Interdisciplinary Perspectives*. Philadelphia: Brunner-Routledge, 1986.

6. Lystad. *Violence in the Home*. 30-36.

7. Perhaps the term "brutishness" is not fittingly ascribed to human agents of wanton violence since, as Dostoevsky has pointed out, human beings are far more cruel than beasts, "so artfully, so artistically cruel." (*The Brothers Karamazov*. The chapter "Rebellion" documents Ivan Karamazov's case for this claim).

8. Lystad. *Violence in the Home*. xiii.

10. See Yale monograph "Frustration and Aggression" (1937) cited in May. *Power and Innocence*. 135.

11. Levinas. "Command and Freedom" in *Collected Philosophical Papers*. 15-23. 16.

12. Young males who have been victimized have experienced the world as a system of power in which sex and power function as the effective weapons of control. So those who have been abused are more likely to take up violence as a means of combating their feelings of powerlessness and victimization. The victim learns to escape abuse by absorbing the logic of the system, emulating the victimizer, and assuming his "rightful turn" at domination. Primo Levi notes the tendency of Auschwitz prisoners to become corrupted by the system that oppresses them, learning to survive by taking up the all-too-clear logic of the system and deploying its cruel methods on fellow prisoners. See *Survival in Auschwitz*. New York: Simon and Schuster, 1996. Note how this syndrome resonates with Bloch's account of the Merina of Madagascar in *From Blessing to Violence*.

13. This is the subject of Rollo May's treatment of violence, *The Power of Innocence*.

14. I have noted that the structure of the household—its easy closure—suits the propagation of myths justifying violence.

15. William Stacey, Anson Shupe. *The Family Secret*. Boston: Beacon Press, 1983. 24.

16. Girard. *Violence and the Sacred*. Chapter 1.

Chapter 8

Superstructures of Identity

Nous brûlons de désir de trouver une assiette ferme
et une dernière base constant
pour y edifier une tour qui s'élève à l'infini;
mais tout notre fondement craque,
et la terre s'ouvre jusqu'aux abîmes.
(Pascal, from "Misere de l'Homme sans Dieu")

We have seen that domestic violence occurs largely as a result of the suffocating enclosure of households that effects a disconnection of the group from the critical social gaze, and also from the reaches of the law and protective authorities that might otherwise intervene to rescue the victims. We have also seen that that disconnection effects a convenient stage for the construction of twisted mythologies that establish the "rightness" of the status quo of power and the "innocence" of the abuser, so that violence is successfully justified and then repeated over lifetimes and even across generations. We have also noted that households, like all economic and political institutions, are ordered ranking systems logically consistent in their structure to the earliest ritualized communities established by our most distant forbears. They still function through the successful imposition of social, economic, legal and political inequalities held in place by the society's ritual systems (social, economic, legal and political).

Persistent, time-honoured, obsessively conservative rituals are most effective in the composition and maintenance, over vast expanses of time, of societies in which people become increasingly committed to the norms of a system that, contrary to Marx's claims, do not simply reflect the ideals, fears, aspirations and goals of the system's power nodes but reflect and embody the ideological forces of the system, detached from the ontological vision or ideological project of any distinct human agent.[1] It is this driving logic, disconnected from personal human agency, that we come designate by the term "bureaucracy."

It is an irony pervasive to Western ways of envisioning perfection (ways, again, consistent with ancient ritualized models of perfection) that we treasure our systems as embodiments of current ideals and visions of perfection despite their always already prior constitution in response to historical circumstances entirely alien to our own. It is equally ironic that we by and large consider ourselves passionately "democratic," fully cognizant of the injustices that social stratifications entail and the frustrations that inequalities incite, and yet we cannot see the faultiness of the ideals of order and integrity that underpin our systems and oblige those inequalities.

It is true that all inequalities involve violences that frustrate healthy human engagement. Yet inequalities are inherent in our "ordered" systems. All systems are, to some degree at least, oppressive, repressive bodies, ordered hierarchies of domination and subordination, homogenizing through expulsion and marginalization, sapping strength from the afflicted and the downtrodden. The scene of homogeneous identity can be ugly when households "order" their internal parts and suppress conflicted differences. I have suggested that indignities and injustice may be felt most deeply in the familial home where one intuitively expects protection and nurturance. But murders and mutilations of hopes and dreams and talents and bodies are dreadful wherever they occur, and a simple corpse-count cannot rate, on a scale of horror, the infinite uniqueness of each particular degradation in the vast array of horrors that people are made to endure. However, when identity work is carried on in massive superstructures of identity according to imagined commonalities, when self-realization is driven by goals of greatness or agendas of vengeance (often "under orders" from supernatural powers), they may thrust themselves onto the world stage with a frightening obsessiveness. Then, the vastness of the destruction that accompanies their glorified missions can exceed the reckoning of our worst nightmares.

In many parts of the world today, the hard coinage of empirical data teaches people it is a harsh, cruel alienating world. Social scientists witness that feelings of detachment, apathy, impotence, and resentment abound in modern times. It is difficult to break through the unyielding shell of greedy self-enclosure spawned by the parched ideals of capitalism. There is little relief from the isolation to be found in the intimacy of the family dwelling, now that the traditionally rich web of familial relations has eroded to an emotionally economical "nuclear" state. People in the modern era, even those not driven from their homes by poverty, hunger, disease, war, or state terrorism, all too often live lives of "homeless" wandering in an ethical wasteland, feeling the truth of their myths of abandonment to a hostile godless planet.

To combat the suffocating enclosure and to find ourselves as "human" again, we venture out of the family dwelling and into the community of humanity, seeking others of "our kind." But the modern world is more than ever a place of terrifying differences. The flux of strange faces and the chaos of opinions and moral attitudes that characterize modern societies do little to ease the sense of detachment. People frantically scan the human landscape for marks of commonality, desiring to connect with others who are "like me," to forge bonds of familiarity and reduce the alienating strangeness of the world. People search for sites of belonging amidst differences they find hostile and threatening. It is true that most people deplore chaos and yearn for the binding grace of consensus. But it is equally true that most of us desire a consensus in which our own voices are dominant, a consensus in which our own loyalties are the most powerfully represented. As Pascal has noted, in the passage cited at the opening of this chapter, we do not simply desire *"une assiette ferme et une dernière base constant"* but we also want *"edifier une tour qui s'élève à l'infini."* It is true that a firm foundation helps us know who we are in a confusing world of differences, but it is equally the case that most prefer the camaraderie of "la tour" to the fraternity of the ghetto.

Belonging within a household is comforting and meaning-giving but belonging within superstructures of identity can give one a powerful sense of importance in the world, a sense of "rightness" and "justness." Larger identity structures—figurations of power coalescing according to perceived commonalities of meaning and aspiration and authorization—can be gathered around religious, tribal/ethnic, political or national self-definitions. Superstructures of identity, by virtue of their mere size or on the basis of longevity, often enjoy a sense of unqualified legitimacy fixed around symbols and "truths" claiming special relations with the divine, illustrious histories or even humiliating histories calling for revenge of past injustices.

Flags, uniforms, anthems, pledges of allegiance to the "fatherland," special languages, secret codes within languages, symbolic foods, sacred signs, social stratifications, glorified narratives, tales of heroes, real or imagined pasts of powerful allegiances or savage injustices requiring retribution—myths and rituals arise around such powerful symbols and become identifying marks of the group. The structure of a social amalgam and its (mythical/ritual) symbols are mutually reinforcing. Psychiatrist May warns:

> The capacity to create and deal with symbols, actually a superb achievement, also accounts for the fact that we are the cruelest species on the planet. We kill not out of necessity but out of allegiance to such symbols as the flag and the fatherland. We kill on principle. [2]

In the modern era, we are witnessing the rise of many new structures of identity, equally passionate in their projects to "self-realize" and "self-determine," whether super in size or small and struggling. This is found counterintuitive by many modern minds, who had expected the close of the Cold War to bring an end to particularisms and usher in an era of global fraternity, since it also dissolved the broad ideological conflicts between communist and democratic ideals of community and politics that had cleaved the world into two distinct and discrete camps. [3] The close of the Cold War did bring an end to any real challenge of global ideological hegemony from Marxist opposition. But the collapse of the two distinct ideological camps also meant the end of an era of distinct political identities wherein it had been a simple matter to locate one's ideological home and distinguish it from the camp of the enemy. After 1989, the opposing "other" had grown more abstract, more diffuse. As a result, identifying oneself and one's comrades among threatening differences became far more difficult. Thus self-definitions began to focus around particularized criteria and conflicts began to have more to do with localized identities within specific warring areas than with grand and pervasive recognizable ideological differences.

In fact, with the diminishing fear of a global and species-threatening conflict, political scientists began to warn of a more insidious oppression rising up within the democratic home, the silent and invisible tyranny of the bureaucracy of the modern state. Hannah Arendt, in *On Violence*, laments:

> the latest and perhaps the most formidable form of domination: bureaucracy or the rule of an intricate system of bureaus in which no men, neither one nor the best, neither the few nor the many, can be held responsible, and which could properly be called rule by Nobody. (If in accord with traditional political thought, we identify tyranny as government that is not held to give an account of itself, rule by Nobody is clearly the most tyrannical of all, since there is no one left who could even be asked to answer for what is being done).[4]

When systems grow so powerful that their logic overwhelms individual goals and desires, we speak of "bureaucracy" to designate the non-human forces—the socio-politico-economic rituals—that drive the ship of state. To feel threatened by the faceless is terrifying. However, a far worse tyranny threatens the autonomy of the citizens of the state, when the logic of the system so fully takes over and dictates goals and desires that the apathetic pawns in their arena do not even recognize themselves to be tyrannized at all. This is what Levinas refers to as the "servile soul."[5]

On the other hand, I believe that Arendt's fears with regard to bureaucracy comprise a localized variant of a grander anxiety that developed in the last half of the twentieth century, an anxiety that had not quite emerged into focus when *On Violence* was written in the 1960s. That anxiety reified in the post-Cold War era. It is the impossibility, as the "menace" of communism receded, of identifying a distinct enemy that made suddenly difficult the localization of responsibility for evils that occurred in the world. When enemies are clear and distinct, good and bad is easily polarized into "us" and "them" and sense can be made of the chaos of existence. But when the enemy disappears and we are left to face the differences within the homespace, identity work becomes thorny and complicated, and every face of friend and enemy alike can loom demonically before us.[6]

The end of the superpower stand-off, thought to usher in a new age of global "human" fraternity that would be manifest in political tranquility and economic rationality, had been expected to render obsolete petty particularisms.

Instead, however, open conflict between smaller non-"state" groups has flared in frequency and ferocity. To understand the transformed threat from battling superpowers to localized ethnic/religious conflict and its correlative global terrorisms, it is necessary to analyze the new threat of "ethnic" violence. I shall allow my discourse to be guided by two excellent treatments of the problem of ethnic conflict: Jack David Eller's *From Culture to Ethnicity to Conflict* (1999) and Kenneth Christie's *Ethnic Conflict, Tribal Politics: A Global Perspective* (1998).

The principal legitimate actors on the world stage at this moment in human history are states. Our maps define the borders of states—not ethnic regions, religious zones or tribal territories. By definition, states are multi-ethnic, multi-religioned and multi-racial gatherings of people inside geographically drawn boundaries. The task of the state then is to amalgamate differences, to merge independent groups of people into a single unit whose identity horizons are not local but coextensive with the state. This requires, at least to a certain extent, the effacement of internal differences and the creation of a state identity. In the United States this drive toward unification is imaged as "the melting pot," a phrase that unabashedly admits its mission as the dissolving of differences.[7] It is the internal violence indicated by this phrase that motivates Emmanuel Levinas to assert that, though a state is born of a "commitment of freedom in the very name of freedom,"[8] the state soon violates the very freedom that gave rise to it. Levinas states:

[T]he commands of written law, the impersonal reason of institutions, despite their origin in free will, become in a certain way alien to the will, which is at every second renewed. Institutions obey a rational order in which freedom no longer recognizes itself.[9]

That is to say, systems are hyper-conservative, sustaining cultural meanings and logical connections from a time out of cultural mind. Bequeathed from a prior-constituted world that is culturally removed from present circumstances by a plethora of historical changes, traditions maintain a sacred tenacity over the modes of being practiced by a people. They maintain this hold through the rituals of the system, through the symbols and ideological underpinnings that give "world" instead of chaos. States may pretend to respect and protect the freedom of its citizen members by supplying them with a stable site for self-actualization. But what does self-actualization mean where histories have always already shaped themselves through us and around us, where histories are serving up the parameters of our possibilities in its prior definitions of "world?" For Levinas, the state, from the moment of its inception, betrays its good intentions in the rigidity of the laws, constitutions and decrees meant as the guarantors of freedom.

"Nation" is a more diffuse term than "state" because, where the unity claimed by a state is entirely illusional and imposed, a nation draws together people who consciously perceive themselves connected through a breadth of identifying features, some real though many imaginary. Anthony Smith in *National Identity* defines nations as:

> named human populations sharing a historic territory, common myths and historical memories, a mass public culture, a common economy and common legal rights and duties for all members.[10]

Eller gives a more general, less embracing definition. He asserts that a nation is "a fully mobilized or institutionalized ethnic group."[11] This definition indicates that what a nation requires above all else is a consciousness of national identity. Eller's definition also suggests that nationhood is achieved when an ethnic group comes to recognize and emphasize territorial and historical qualifications over physical or racial ones. A nation will perceive its commonalities in traditional cultural practices within a defined territorial space. Its members will probably embrace a common mythological history and share "cultural memories" (real or imagined). They often share beliefs in rights and responsibilities and delineate common norms in cultural prescriptions and prohibitions.

If a nation manages to organize polity around these common identifying features and achieve statehood, then the "nation-state" emerges. This form of state has long been the model and the aspiration of Western national entities. For at least the last two centuries, it has provided the dominant social model in Europe and, more recently, it has been the ideal of socio-political organization around the globe, though very few actual states can boast the degree of ethnic purity that would warrant their calling themselves nation-states. The perceived commonalities are all too often fictions in the minds of individuals feeling overwhelmed and threatened by their socio-economico-political environments, and their call for a binding identity often comprises a cry for rights and power.

Tribes are essentially identical with ethnic groups. They are no less civilized and certainly not as destructive as nation-states.[12] Yet there is a tendency in general parlance to use the term "tribal" to designate a phenomenon where one disapproves of it and to use "ethnic" if one is being less judgmental. What this indicates is that the term "tribe" has gained a connotation of lawlessness and anarchy. Tribes are generally viewed, following the usual pattern of demonization, as operating at a high level of internal organization and uniformity (exaggeratedly potent) and as prone to conflict due to a diminished tolerance for outsiders (exaggeratedly threatening). The general prejudice is that tribes have especially clear identity markers and practice especially strong rituals of inclusion and exclusion.

However, all ethnic groups emphasize commonalities and practice rituals that consolidate and assert the identity of the group. Many will be exclusionary because their very survival in many instances will depend upon their obsessive practice of common social rituals and their withdrawal and isolation from other, often larger, more culturally powerful identity groups. The term "tribal politics," then, generally tells us less about a group's geographical criteria or developmental methodology, than it tells about the observer's faithfulness to ritualized understandings of difference. We feel more threatened by the differences of the economically and politically underdeveloped world of post-colonial Africa and India, so we call their conflicts "tribal." When we speak of tensions in white Western lands, like Ireland, the Balkans and Canada, we say "ethnic." However, if the term tribal is generally used to designate savagery and barbarism, if it suggests reversion to a more primitive, less "civilized" state, then certainly the overwhelming majority of ethnic conflicts around the world deserve to be addressed as "tribal."

Ethnic groups will often allege long, continuous histories of cultural distinctness, distinctness often claimed as earned in (glorious) war. These claims confer upon the group a commonality that assumes "rights" as a singular people, though, again, very few ethnic groups truly qualify for this distinction (of a long and continuous history or of distinction in glorious war). In actuality, in the modern world, ethnicity can be and often is purely manufactured and exploited for purposes of economic or political self-interest. Often ethnic identities have been reinvented and recharged with new political missions in response to changing local or national pressures.

One thing is clear, however. Ethnicity comprises the ideological grounding for the majority of the world's post-Cold War horrors. There have been repeated genocidal projects and "ethnic cleansing" operations all around the globe, employing the cruelest methods of torture, slaughter and exile to expel contaminating elements and purify the ethnic homespace. Across contemporary Eastern Europe, throughout Asia, Africa and the Middle East, there is an endless flow of homeless humanity, the barely surviving dregs refugeed by ethnic hostilities. The degree of global suffering caused by this type of conflict alone is stunning. Kenneth Christie states:

> This type of conflict has produced more abject misery and loss of life than any other in the post second world war period. [13]

One more of the many troubling features of ethnic conflict resides in the inability of borders and even oceans to insulate other societies from the fallout of ethnic wars, since ethnic groups, by definition, do not maintain simply and exclusively within state boundaries. Their hostilities often overflow onto others who then become unsuspecting victims in ethnic wars in which they are not at all "definitively" implicated yet to which they come to add new and further confusing elements.

Hostilities between human groups aligned on the basis of perceived commonalities flood the globe in the modern era. In one, common language may be the identifying focus, in another religion or historical heritage. Whatever the decisive factor or factors for perceived commonality, certainly very few groups are ancient in origin or organically distinct social entities. Many are decidedly recent phenomena. For most, the referents of identity focus or the emphasis upon referents keeps shifting over time. Not all ethnic groups are obsessive in their inclusions and exclusions; many are not isolationist nor pathologically defensive. The conflicts that do maintain between ethnic groups are not equal in intensity, longevity or ferocity. Even the goals of ethnic conflicts can be widely diverse in nature. The span of features called upon to distinguish the group can be so broad that it has led Eller to name the concept of ethnicity one of the most "elastic" of identity terms.[14]

What the definition of ethnicity is taken to be or how ethnicity is different from tribalism matters less than the salience and effectiveness of the term in social discourse. The term permits the concentration of power around collective goals that makes possible the articulation of demands for political or economic rights that would otherwise be diffuse and inexpressible. Trond Gilberg has suggested that much ethnic particularism is no more than a simple "identity excuse" for self-serving groups to atomize in order to practice a sheer "hooliganism" and "organized criminality."[15] Since ethnicity has proven politically expedient, it is used as a common defense for illegal and anti-state violence. Gilberg is suspicious that, in the Balkans for example, ethnic claims are used to mask what are simply the latest episodes in a long-standing tradition of banditry.

Perhaps the most compelling claim of Trond Gilberg's important treatment of ethnic conflict is his elucidation of the long term effects of histories of conflict and corruption. Gilberg explains that, when brigands and freedom fighters become tomorrow's leaders and bring corruption into state-wide practice (as is so often the actual consequence of ethnic uprisings), criminal behavior patterns can emerge in the culture at large that are almost impossible to dislodge. When organized criminality comprises the official code, it soon becomes a feature of ordinary business practice and, then, a factor of daily life across the population. Changes in government can be rapid and frequent in corrupted societies but political change can rarely erase the long term cultural effects of corrupted social values. This is because, as we have seen, cultural truths are doggedly conservative. So changes in the power nodes of the society can only rarely bring decisive change to the governing logic that rules the system, let alone to the ethical beliefs or social customs practiced by the community.

Before leaving the problem of ethnic conflict, it is important that we take note of one special form of "ethnic" threat, the one posed by groups gathered around religious belief. Religious identities are especially dangerous and conflicts between rival groups are the bloodiest of all ethnic hostilities, because the religious worldview is so structurally faithful to the ontological messages of ritual and myth. Their symbols and logic compress ideological assertions (such as the "two-worlds" theory) that sanction ordering violences. Religious identity is also dangerous because that identity is built upon claims of special relations with the divine, and gods may give to individuals, church authorities, or state leaders transcendental authorization for the most brutal and cruel acts. The sense of self-righteousness, the certainty surrounding "myths of innocence," and the passionate, unquestioning loyalty to the god's cause can configure purgative missions expelling infidel contaminants more zealous and thus more violent than any other type of undertaking.

All religious orders comprise powerful forces in the cultural imaginary of their followers because they supply the symbolic and emotional resources needed to sustain control over populations over changing historical circumstances. Religions, whether macrocosmic superpower or microcosmic cult, develop elaborate, sophisticated, emotionally powerful, expressive and iconic traditions, rich in symbolic texture. They compose elaborate ritual systems that ideologically embrace and configure even simple daily acts like eating and speaking. There will be secret codified greetings, special music, emotionally-charged testimonial rites, confessional and other purgative ceremonies, punitive procedures (often systematized, sometimes self-inflicted), and programs of awards for the faithful (often in a transcendental gift system). Older, worldwide religions are imbued with the authority of centuries and millennia of obsessively regulated practice. Their mythical and ritual histories run deep in the cultural bodies of much of the present world. But most religious structures, whatever their longevity and size, have deeply installed narrative expressions of their "rightness," myths affirming their "singular" relation with the god and notions of a special divine calling and transcendental authorization to pursue that mission with appropriate fervour.

All religious orders come complete with political agendas, whether overtly displayed or cunningly concealed. Many are highly influential in the political arena of states and the world because of the great power they represent in their flourishing numbers. Religious structures have great weight in the world because they own and operate the scales by which social realities and individuals come to be measured. Thus they stand in a strong position to generate and define grievances that spawn collective activism. The religious mindset is always poised toward the political, as Bloch has indicated.[16] Christian Smith has persuasively argued that religious orders encourage an "insurgent consciousness" in their adherents. Religious doctrines, positing transcendent "more perfect" worlds, illuminate the "fallenness" of this world. Often the world is depicted in religious discourse as egregiously violating eternal moral standards. Thus, religious believers can easily be pressed into collective destructions to purge evil and right the wrongs of this world. Individuals too stand at risk if they question religious motives or actions. Disbelievers can easily be judged by the god's soldiery and found morally wanting.

Religious belief more or less explicitly encourages pathologies of defense and hysterias for cleanliness from the polluting elements of a "fallen" world. Fanatics have always measured devotion by how hard and how long one is willing to fight for what he believes. This is the reason why holy wars are the bloodiest and most brutal of all conflicts. James A. Aho tells:

> The enhancement of the spiritual in the cult of the transcendent god and the relative devaluation of the material world lend plausibility to the separation of absolute ends from material means, of the telic and the ethical from the practical and utilitarian aspects of economics, politics and war. It makes credible the

experience of military violence as work, serving an end apart from and higher than itself.[17]

Since religion's aims are thought to be "apart from and higher than" worldly ends, arguments of suffering as byproducts to religious "work" bear little weight for the believer. Holy wars communicate the rage of the god against a "fallen" humanity. That perception alone requires that the holy war be waged with ample fury.

Perhaps in the case of the religious entity, more than any other kind of "ethnic" grouping, there is direct evidence of ritual's ontologies and ideologies in the ossified patterns of thinking and behavior that legitimate violence. "Pathologies of defense" that demonize the different and provide "idioms of conquest" are clearly in evidence in religious orders. Religious identity structures are by definition sanctified homespaces, consecrated by the god. Evil is easily projected upon the alien by virtue of the fact of the infidel's inassimilability. Desmond Morris asserts that religious identity comprises a "culturally isolating mechanism that demands social separation from those who worship in a different manner."[18] James A. Aho emphasizes, in terms more resonant with ritual, religion's obsessiveness about contamination by outsiders.

> As a rule in Judaism, Islam and Protestantism, responsibility for the world's sin is projected onto minority populations, strangers and foreigners: those with tongues and customs and pantheons alien to God's faithful. In collectively objectifying evil and positing it upon that external enemy, a sense of cleanliness of His "remnant" is created symbolically.[19]

It is striking how Aho's language resonates with the anthropologists' accounts of scapegoating and countercultural rejection. Compare his observations with Mary Douglas' account of primitive rituals of purification:

> Eliminating dirt is not a negative movement, but a positive effort to organize the environment...Rituals of purity and impurity create unity in experience...The society does not exist in a neutral uncharged environment...that which is not with it, part of it and subject to its laws is potentially against it. [20]

When we think upon the collective histories of religious organizations in the world, we don't know whether to blame the bloodshed and the horror on the gods whose divine plans necessitated them, or on the species that invented the gods. Either way, we are likely to agree with Dostoevsky's criticism, placed in the mouth of Ivan Karamazov:

> The marvel is that such an idea, the idea of the necessity of God, could enter the head of such a savage, vicious beast as man.[21]

This "savage, vicious beast," in the name of his god, has machine-gunned Muslims knelt in prayer in their mosques (Sri Lanka 1990, Israeli West Bank 1994), stoned to death women suspected of adultery (Somalia 1993, Pakistan 1991), chopped arms and legs off social offenders (Pakistan 1991), publicly beheaded people for "insulting god" (Saudi Arabia 1992), murdered abortion clinic doctors (Oregon 1993), collapsed the World Trade Center killing thousands of innocent civilians (New York 2001) and now bombs Afghani children. Religion is a powerful force in human events and religious fanaticism is by far the greatest "ethnic" threat to peace in the world today.

There is little doubt that obsessions with identity are the driving force that terrorizes most of the globe. It is the driving force of the "new world disorder" as Alexander Johnston has so aptly phrased the post-Cold War situation.[22] Communal loyalties on the basis of perceived commonalities are the rallying point for ethno-national projects around the globe seeking capture and control of their state apparatuses. This is a fully logical and predictable outcome of the passion for ordered community, evidenced in the hyperbolic identity rhetoric that celebrates self-determination as a "natural right" of peoples. A fervent emotionalism often attaches to essentialist identity politics and drives people, on the basis of often illusional histories or fictions of a special destiny, toward projects of military take-over or missions of "justified" revenge for past injustices.

Ethnic groups are composed of individuals who "find themselves" by identifying with others and discovering solidarity and belonging by reference to powerful symbolisms and meanings. Ethnicity is consciousness of a sameness with others equally motivated to define themselves and mobilize to achieve a socially organized intimacy—a "kinship experience." Whatever the claims of commonality within the group, ethnic definitions are always, to some extent, mere labels attached to detached beings to create a sense of community in a threatening and isolating world, labels that serve administrative and practical purposes as well as clearly existential ones. The obsession for belonging is perhaps the most necessary factor for people's healthy co-dwelling, and it is also perhaps the most dangerous force active in the world today. It can only be eased by providing people with a sense of belonging, a sense of social connectedness, and healthy, safe, meaningful ways of realizing and expressing their singularity.

This is why the image of the "melting pot" is so entirely faulty as a national ideal. It seeks to replace "kinship" notions with the cold fraternity of mass society by obliterating the differences essential to self-definition. To treat humans as equals (not to be misconstrued as treating people "equitably"[23]), a prized "democratic" principle, is to think individuals interchangeable—"meltable" into one another. It is to suppress the uniqueness of their desires, motivations, aspirations, needs and sufferings, to deny them their dignity as singular beings. Dignity reposes in differences, not in the faceless equality of interchangeability. When differences are denied, ethnic fanaticisms may have an enormous draw for those feeling "interchangeable."

Whether all minorities will be rapidly absorbed in a faceless global mass society or whether each will be forced down a separatist road; whether the world can learn to appreciate the rich possibilities for social encounter on the basis of difference rather than commonality; whether true "community of humanity" outside of insipid homogeneity can occur in any site that is not a battlefield; whether peaceful engagement among diverse beings remains a human possibility, given the histories of violence behind us and the ritualized patterns of engagement that set directions of future encounter—all these remain to be seen. In a world of radical political and economic inequalities that leave painful gaps in global justice, the rhetoric of "global community" and the "brotherhood" of the species rings as empty in modern ears as the ancient tales of monster-gods thrashing out justice from the chaos, or the utopian propaganda of "common wealth" inherited from the noblest classical philosophies.

Notes

1. These fears and hopes are always already preconfigured in response to historical situations whose political, economic and social forces are no longer in play.

2. Rollo May. *Power and Innocence*. 156.

3. It has remained an endless source of self-congratulations in the West that societies whose revolutions were inspired by Marxist utopian visions of liberty from history collapsed as the dystopias of the modern era. These self-congratulations notwithstanding, the failure of Marxist states around the globe was a function of a faulty understanding of history, as Maurice Bloch has persuasively argued. The failure of Marxist-inspired utopian states might better be attributed to the impossibility of any new order beginning in a political and economic vacuum, rather than to specific shortcomings in the utopian vision. In *From Blessing to Violence*, Bloch demonstrates that theories that predict certain outcomes to history on the assumption of a simple, punctual historical creation are grounded in a false notion of history, a "pseudo-history" that assumes "an absolute beginning when a thinker, unbound by society or the necessities of life or for that matter any previous intellectual conceptions, worked out the whole thing." (See *From Blessing to Violence*. 5-11). Since histories never begin at a zero baseline, the real communist movements that tried to transplant their ideals in an already rapidly industrializing, modernizing world were all very much nationalistic movements from their beginnings. Marxist hopefuls were obliged to history the moment they tried to institute their programs in real existing states. They soon discovered that the lofty ideals of communism were not transplantable in those societies because the ethic of the Marxist utopian vision could only be undermined by the actual fervencies of nationalisms in their individual historical contexts. Communists could not hope to replace *in toto* the ontological and ideological assumptions in place in the society wherein they attempted to institute their reforms. In other words, communist ideals could not alter the overarching logic firmly established in the society's institutions. They could not reconstruct current worldviews nor alter the general mindset of the "common mental world" no matter how lofty their guiding ideals. Nor could communist ideals fend off the onslaught of its most seductive enemy, capitalist greed. Western culture is itself a "commodity" fast being exported throughout the entire world. Its overarching and governing values, individualism and autonomy, offer irresistible economic and political arguments against the fundamental communist ideal of shared common wealth. With the rise of international markets and with national servitude to the

latter, only the richest of nations, the imperial powers, had the independence, autonomy and the economic mastery to survive the new demands and pressures in order to compete in the global setting. The economic giants that already reigned could retain an economic independence of which the smaller, struggling states could barely dream. In a world that offers opportunity only to the few who already have, and degradation to the many who can never hope to compete, the ideals of "common good" and "broadly shared wealth" that underpin the communist utopian vision appeal only to the powerless who do not have the force to apply them. Unless Marxists could convince the have's to share, nationally and globally, the project was not going to get off the ground.

4. Hannah Arendt. *On Violence.* 38-39.

5. Emmanuel Levinas. "Freedom and Command" in *Collected Philosophical Papers.* 15-24.

6. Compare to Girard's "sacrificial crisis," wherein rival identities collapse into one other causing the conceptual order of the social unit to topple. (*Violence and the Sacred.* Chapter 2).

7. Not all states find blameless this drive to efface individual identity and replace it with homogeneity. For example, the social metaphor employed in Canada, the "mixed salad," conveys an image that is less totalizing in intent than the "mixed salad" metaphor of the United States.

8. Levinas. "Freedom and Command" in *Collected Philosophical Papers.* 15-24.

9. Levinas. "Freedom and Command." 17.

10. Anthony Smith. *National Identity.* Reno: University of Nevada, 1991. 40.

11. Jack David Eller. *From Culture to Ethnicity to Conflict.* 17.

12. Kenneth Christie. *Ethnic Conflict, Tribal Politics: A Global Perspective.* 8.

13. Christie. *Ethnic Conflict, Tribal Politics.* 1-2.

14. Eller. *From Culture.* 8.

15. "Ethnic Conflict in the Balkans" in *Ethnic Conflict, Tribal Politics: A Global Perspective.* 61-85.

16. Bloch. *Prey into hunter.* 6.

17. James A. Aho. *Religious Mythology and the Art of War.* Westport, Conn.: Greenwood Press, 1981. 191.

18. Desmond Morris. *The Naked Ape.* New York: Harry N. Abrams Inc., 1977. 149.

19. Morris. *The Naked Ape.* 151.

20. Mary Douglas. *Purity and Danger: an analysis of the concepts of Pollution and Taboo.* New York & London: Routledge, 1984. 4.

21. F. Dostoevsky. *The Brothers Karamazov.* 216.

22. Christie. *Ethnic Conflict, Tribal Politics.* 129-152. c.f. 147-149.

23. The "democratic" principle of equalization that mediocritizes diverse people is criticized *ad nauseam* by Nietzsche. (*The Genealogy of Morals, Beyond Good and Evil*).

Chapter 9

In the Wake of Violent Rituals

*Of the other tears of humanity with which the earth is soaked from its crust to
its center, I will say nothing...
But then there are the children,
and what am I to do about them?*
(voiced by Ivan Karamazov in *The Brothers Karamazov*)[1]

Primitive gods may have retired long ago, but we may, in our daily interactions
with others, continue to keep the faith. We may still mark out the sacred from
the profane spaces of the gods' domain, punish and reward on their behalf. We
may still call upon powerful rituals to "order" our sacred homespaces and expel
the contaminating forces. Languages, virtues, values and ideologies, social systems, traditions and institutions are formed of mythical symbols and bound by
ritual logic. They have made for a world replete with violence at every locale of
social encounter and every level of identity. From the household to the churches
to the houses of parliament to the international courts of justice, we define who
we are by opposing ourselves to different others. The degree to which we see
otherness as "monstrous" and witness our fellows as "evil" marks the degree to
which we remain faithful to the logic of violent rituals and repeat the histories of
species violences.

    What is diabolical is not that our fellows are morally fallen. What is dia-
bolical is that we believe that we have a god's-eye view on their moral collapse.
What is diabolical is that we believe that the moralizing gesture of witnessing
his "fall" grants expiation from the crimes of humanity. But the stark reality of
the "human condition" is that most of us are both good and evil, in some ways
"elevated" and in others sadly "fallen." Our innocence and our guilt are both
myth and fact, illusional and real. All "homespaces" are both sacred and monstrous. The stark fact of the matter is that evil is an altogether common and very

"human" phenomenon. It comes to be in famine and flood, in sickness and in ageing, in love and in war. Most evils cannot be separated, let alone purified, from the "human" condition. Those few evils that might be exorcised generally come about as a direct result of the inflexible moral distinctions that assign guilt and contamination to outsiders and relieve the homespace of responsibility for the injustices and abuses of their systems.

Naming atrocities anomalous, naming the perpetrator as mad, naming evil as monstrous does not serve toward ethical being. Concealments of the normalcy of violence shield us from self-examination. But violence is neither abnormal nor aberrant. It is not even perverse (from the evolved habits of the species). It is an altogether mundane "human" event. It is part and parcel of who we are and of what our systems compose. Violence is *in* the cruel circumstances of life and *composes* the taxing frustrations of life, and violence comprises a "reasonable" and adaptive response to those circumstances and frustrations. Whenever we find ourselves at either of the two extremes of human power—either robustly empowered (as Nietzsche and Bloch have shown) or powerless (as May has demonstrated)—we will find ourselves, one and all, prone to murderous engagement with our fellows. It is not the perversions of others that renders our homespaces dangerous. It is those ritualized, moralizing, "elevated," "innocent," pathological responses that grant purified self-definition to our "ordered worlds" by locating the "demon" in others and exorcizing them from our midst.

Given the remarkable persistence of violent rituals in the early history of human communities, one has good reason to suspect, with the anthropologists, that violent ways of being may have seeped into the very materiality of our kind and into our cultural formations. This is not a speculation that could ever bear substantiating proof but it *does* offer an explanation for the gap between our bloody deeds and our ostensibly benevolent intentions. It offers a compelling explanation for the cruel history of species engagement. And it also provides a plausible explanation for the otherwise inexplicable ability of ordinary "decent" folk to remain apathetic and detached in the face of the most brutal acts to others, and even to automatically assume, conscience-free, a role in the most hideous crimes.[2]

We have been educated to expect and to look for coherence and meaning in human behavior. This is Ivan's Karamazov's complaint: there appears to be no "reason" behind the brutalizing events that go on around us, and even less behind the willingness of the participants and the apathy of the onlookers. But, if the anthropologists are correct in their suspicions, then the "reasons" for both human cruelty and our apathy toward the suffering may be located in "truths" lodged more deeply than our conscious minds can reach in seeking out the "reason-able." If bodies are the problem—the fleshy bodies of individuals and the "bodies" of our cultural forms and institutions—then those anthropologists may be correct who suspect that, when it comes to human evolution, only the violent and the selfish survive.[3]

I am proposing that we entertain the dark possibilities raised by the anthropologists in order that we might look within ourselves and within modern modes of engagement for vestiges of destructive behavior patterns. We might seek out, in our ways of being-in-the-world, traces of violence-legitimating ideologies, ontologies that make "righteous" our social and political patterns of domination and oppression, "pathologies of defense" that configure neighbors and strangers as exaggeratedly potent and malevolent, and "idioms of conquest" that sanction aggressive overflow. I am most convinced by the proposition that we still think in terms of stark polar oppositions cast in over-simplified "religious" world-views. This polarization is clearly evident in the nationalistic fervour of Western superpowers that condemn as "terrorists" those who oppose their intrusiveness, disbelieve their "myths of innocence" and resent their economic and political hegemony in the world.

Ontologies persisting deep in the lifeworld may be responsible for these "myths of innocence" and for the facile moral judgments and condemnations of "monstrous" others that flood the public sphere. We may be witnessing directly the effect of our violent histories in the aggressive identity work that is carried out in the world today—in obsessions with "ethnic purity" and the impassioned quest for "homelands." We see it in the evangelical lust of religious groups as they seek to spread "the god's word." We see it in racism, tribalism, and in extremes of gender differencing. We see it in the zealous flares of nationalistic fervour with its "love it or leave it" propaganda that configures internal disagreement as treacherous and external criticism as jealousy or "terrorism." And we see it in the typically Western passion for "order" and coherence, in our ideals of integrity and unity. Violence has triumphed as an ideology to the degree that we see difference as threatening, to the degree we find others "monstrous" and "demonic," and to the degree that moral judgments of our fellows come easily and self-examination comes hard.

Accepting the dark truth about our primal urges and about the logic structuring our ordered systems and configuring our codes of etiquette and propriety may help us to understand our crimes of commission and omission, but can they help us to *change* the human condition? Can our admission that "monstrousness" actually comprises our "civilizing" forces and remains a fundamental feature of our "sacred" homespaces offer any solutions to Ivan's haunting question about the torture and murder of innocents (cited at the opening of this chapter): *What are we to do about the children?* How can we turn our violence-prone faculties toward the healing of a wounded world that is soaked, as Ivan says, from its crust to its center in the tears of a suffering humanity?

There may not be much that we can do—quickly—to alter our fundamental dispositions in favour of violence or our natural thrust toward legitimating violences when we see them occurring in the world. However, I am not proposing here a "biological fatalism." Violence may be encrypted within our bodies and may underpin our systems and institutions but, if the social scientists are correct in their assertion that certain psychic conditions (a sense of helplessness, isolation or threat) trigger the violent responses, there are precautions we can take to protect ourselves and others.

We must be attentive to our own dispositions, knowing ourselves to be prone to facile moralizations that activate pathologies of defense and counter-cultural rejections. But we need also be attentive to the happiness of others around us, knowing that their frustrations can easily burst their fragile seal and overflow onto us all. Tending the wounds of the victimized, helping them to feel empowered and engaged in their worlds, and securing them in safe "homelands" can be a reasonable starting place for calming the aggressive urges and averting outbreaks of violence.

However, in the final analysis, the most truly efficacious response to the problem of human atrocity resides *within* Ivan's question: *What are we to do about the children?* Children provide our most solid hope to alter the moral destiny of the species. We may be old and set in our violent ways, but the children have the time and the openness of mind and body to absorb gentler, kinder ideologies. Socrates states in the *Republic*, that the hope for justice resides with those under ten years of age. All over ten will have to be "sent away" if a just society is to be achieved. However, I suspect that we over-ten-year-old's might still have some purpose to serve in helping to create new, more wholesome rituals, more soothing music for young souls and gentler gymnastics for their bodies. There may still be enough "evolutionary time" to persuade our young against the appropriateness of violence. In fact, social scientists have been telling us for some time that changes *within* generations are rarely achieved, but cross-generational changes can be quite successfully effected. Parents and grandparents, teachers and other adults can have a dramatic impact upon the young, not merely by tending their bodies and nurturing their minds and protecting them from the violences that disfigure their gentility, but by nourishing their love of justice and their sympathies for less fortunate others, and simply by providing gentle, compassionate, non-hyper-moralizing exemplars.

Charles Burke, in his *Aggression in Man*, has written that we, in the West, are currently failing at these important tasks.[4] Ours, he claims, is one of the most aggressive societies on the planet today, markedly continuous, in our methods of rearing and disciplining our children, with the most perversely bellicose tribes practicing war, cannibalism, clitoral mutilations and human sacrifice. Our child-rearing practices, claims Burke, "foster an uncommon number of aggressive impulses."[5] The programming begins in infancy in the wide-sweeping refusal of mothers to breast-feed their babies and in other early frustrations of the child's oral gratification needs. Then daycare and other strangers replace family nurturance so that the American dream can be maintained with as little interruption as possible.

The family nest can, from the outset, be cold and unsatisfying for many, and children can be thrust from that sanctuary long before they are emotionally ready. We tend to discourage dependency in our offspring, asserts Burke, and we begin in infancy to prepare them for their departure into the anonymity of the world. To this end, perhaps unconsciously, we tend toward sufficient harshness in our child-rearing to ensure their (and our) self-sovereignty. After the desired break is achieved and the mere intimations of rejection are substantialized—the teen moves out of the family home freeing the parents from the yoke of parental duty—visiting remains puzzlingly obligatory in the young, while ambivalent in its motivations and its meanings. Even in those rare cases where parents postpone their careers and curb their material lusts to stay and tend their young, this often results in such frustration and resentment that the home can become what Burke calls "a pool of sublimated aggressions."[6]

Burke may exaggerate the case against Western parents, but we cannot deny the general truth of his claims. Our cultures do in fact make absolute the values of autonomy and freedom, and it is quite the norm for many couples to abandon their babies to the care of strangers. Many dissolve their parental responsibility when their children reach their teens. Many fathers in our society (and now, increasingly, mothers) abandon their responsibilities toward their babies from the outset and have to be hunted down and court-ordered to put food in their children's mouths.

We might further add to Burke's argument about the collapse of the nurturing family in the West the fact that, when our elders return to childlike ways and threaten dependency, we tend to shuffle them off to the cold care of strangers in "homes" that are less like homes than waiting rooms to expedite their final departure. This is a glaring social irony in our culture since we can be certain that richer, fuller family units that embrace multiple generations can provide a wider base of support and lessen the frustrations and resentments of parenting. Grandparents often prove *more* effective with our children than parents because of the redoubled cross-generational advantage. And a full family dwelling enlivened by many voices of truth can most naturally foster an appreciation for diversity, undercut the over-seriousness of family disputes and disarm the obsessive authoritarianism that can build up around narrow centers of power.

Burke's criticisms of family life in the West only point toward a more fundamental problem in our societies. It is the faulty ideals that underpin our systems and configure our cultural practices that are the deeper problem for raising healthy human beings. Order and integrity are inadequate *as ideals* for evolving, dynamic beings situated in a multi-cultural, multi-coloured, multi-religioned, multi-racial, multi-vocal world. Freedom and independence and autonomy as guiding principles of self-actualization reassert a view of subjectivity as radically free and unobtruded—not simply a mistaken view of subjectivity, but dangerous as a model.

These ideals need to be replaced with others—gentler, more humble, more responsive, others more appropriate to the healing of a wounded world. Ideals of generosity and compassion can serve in the world at large to tend the victims of atrocities, as well as they can serve in the family dwelling to allow differences to coexist. These can serve as common principles to guide behavior in private homespaces as well as in the world at large, so that there need be no serious gap between our child-rearing methods and our ways of being-in-the-world, no gap between the guiding logic of the home and the school and our guiding principles in the world.

Changing *who* we are by changing *what* we think about ourselves and others and *how* we manifest those thoughts in interaction—the reconstruction of society through a conscious reconstruction of the "common mental world" of our lived experiences—is a monumental task, perhaps impossible when attempted always necessarily from within the locus of prevailing truths. Escaping the "logic" of one's system may be psychically impossible, since possibilities for free rational criticism and moral judgment can barely arise *as possibilities* from within the existing system. Even if a shift in vision were possible, permitting a glimpse into wider possibilities, fighting an inhuman system from within commits the combatant to no less than counter-socialization. It would require the capacity to maintain an active individual conscience over against the general beliefs of the system.

This is not an outright impossibility, but clearly it would take one of Nietzsche's "overmen" to gain a larger perspective on the system in which he is imbedded. And this would be dangerous in two ways. It would be dangerous precisely because, as we have seen, the conscience of the creative artist as well as his driving "vision of perfection" can themselves be violent and oppressive, disconnected as they are from the law and from social critique. And it is dangerous because, even where conscience and vision of perfection remain healthy and morally viable, systems by their very nature have built-in limits to the degree and kind of dissent that they will tolerate. The more rigid the system, the more needful of change, yet the more rigid the limits to dissent.

Grand wholesale schemes for relaxing rigid systems to allow for the necessary critique that would effect the necessary changes would also require a full scale social transformation of the members of the social group—both those in power and, as we have seen, those most oppressed by the system. This fact points toward the self-frustrating and paradoxical proposition that nothing short of a mass psychic conversion of society is required to effect social and systematic change. That is, societies need to be changed in order for societies to be changed! It is true that our societies need to be changed. The values that underpin them and the self-righteous arrogance that express those values are dangerous in the world. Changes from within the system will come only slowly, if they come at all.

If people within offending systems *could* address the deep structural flaws within the economic and political sectors of their systems, they could insist upon an entire reorientation of the offending sectors of their orders. They could insist upon the full inclusion of the poor and the oppressed in all benefits of the system. They could call for reasonable restraints upon the overzealous authorities that force homogeneity upon the diverse population. But every society relies upon a dialectic of inclusion and exclusion to establish a sense of identity and worth. There is always, *indigenous* to systems, the propensity to identify one's own social allies as good and to project evil upon "monstrous" others. This cannot appear as un-*reason*-able within the lifeworld of living beings because reason is a tool employed regularly and successfully in the domination of people and nature. Justice fails because reason fails as an instrument of justice. Reason fails because, as Levinas has shown, its computations do not reach the ethical dimension of things.

If we *could* break free of our violating systems successfully enough to see the hollowness of their claims of sacred purity and unqualified legitimacy, we would surely accept the argument of the anthropologists that the domain of violence coextends with the over-determined assembly of powers and forces that we know as the "human world." There exists no purified realm cut loose from the orchestrations of violence. The entire terrain of human engagement— linguistic, social, political and economic—is coextensive with the "monstrousness" it condemns in its alienated others. The proud claim of the "civilization" of the species, upon which conceptual basis the "civilized" have historically oppressed and enslaved their more "primitive" neighbors, has been a cruel hoax all along. If the species has progressed at all, in the millennia since the first of our ancestors stood upright and walked onto the savannah, it has only advanced in its ability to fashion new and ever more deceptive "religious" concealments to mask the "grotesque and inexpedient" aggressiveness peculiar to our species and the injustices upon which human systems rest, by which the "legitimate" prosper, and under whose grip the marginal still suffer.

What are the chances that our systems will evolve to address the needs of the forgotten and the oppressed? What are the chances that our children will know a more just world than our historical worlds have proven? Like the anthropologists, I am pessimistic. I believe that the chances of positive change are slim. The value of the happiness of the relieved sufferer will always be weighed against the benefits to the donor. And, since around the globe the scales of justice are owned and operated exclusively by the donors, and never by the sufferers, the necessity to change the gross inequalities that underpin our "ordered" systems will always be gauged by a rational calculation made by those who have something to lose, for the sake of those who have nothing to offer. The starving, the homeless, the displaced, and the downtrodden have no utility, no value— only needs. The only function they perform resides *in* their identity as the "demonic" through which they serve our identity work. They serve as the "monstrous" backdrop against which our "sacred" homespaces can be constructed.

Notes

1. F. Dostoevsky. *The Brothers Karamazov*. 224.

2. Hannah Arendt's *Eichmann in Jerusalem: A Report on the Banality of Evil* was found scandalous by many of her fellow Jews precisely because it pointed out that their own religious leaders were instrumental in rounding up the people to be sent off to their torture and deaths. It was the normalcy of these participations, the ease with which average persons took up their places in the chain of atrocities that Arendt was concerned to emphasize. Similarly, Karl Jaspers notes the common passivity in the face of radical evil

in his *The Question of German Guilt*. He chides: "But each one of us is guilty in so far as he remained inactive. The guilt of passivity is difficult. Impotent excuses; no moral law demands a spectacular death. . . . But passivity knows itself morally guilty of every failure, every neglect to act whenever possible, to shield the imperiled, to relieve the wrong, to countervail."

3. Walter Burkert reminds us: "It is the genes, not the individuals, that get passed on; hence it is the cheater within the group who enjoys the greater advantage and by this very fitness will multiply his genes." An even less palatable observation from the anthropological community asserts that killing and the consequent distribution of meats so pervasive in the early millennia of the species can be observed even within chimpanzee groups. This raises the possibility that the rituals practiced by early human communities for thousands of years before they developed speech may have been bequeathed across genetic boundaries. The ethological perspective holds that the selective process that advantages the ethically unobtruded has been functioning for thousands upon thousands of generations. (See Walter Burkert. *Homo Necans*. I.2., n.23. for a full bibliography of this claim.)

4. As parents, asserts Burke, we actually teach our children hatred and hostility. Many of our cultural practices, from the hyper-masculinity of its Christian imagery to the super-moral bravado of its cultural and cinematic heroes, reflect the dangerous orientation of our Western cultures. However, it is primarily our child-rearing practices that teach violence to our offspring. (Secaucus, N.J.: Lyle Stuart Inc., 1975).

5. Burkert. *Homo Necans*. 173.

6. Burkert. *Homo Necans*. 173.

Selected Bibliography

Bloch, Maurice. *From Blessing to Violence: History and Ideology in the Circumcision Ritual of the Merina of Madagascar*. Cambridge. U. K.: Cambridge University Press, 1986.

———. *Prey into hunter: The Politics of Religious Experience*. Cambridge. U. K.: Cambridge University Press, 1992.

Burke, Charles. *Aggression in Man*. Secaucus, N. J.: Lyle Stuart Inc., 1975.

Burkert, Walter. *Creation of the Sacred: Tracks of Biology in Early Religions*. Cambridge, Mass.: Harvard University Press, 1996.

———. *Homo Necans: An Anthropology of Ancient Greek Sacrificial Ritual and Myth*. tr. Peter Bing. Berkeley: University of California Press, 1983.

———. *Structure and History in Greek Myth and Ritual*. Berkeley, Calif.: University of California Press, 1979.

Christie, Kenneth, ed. *Ethnic Conflict, Tribal Politics: A Global Perspective*. Surrey, U.K.: Curzon Press, 1998.

Daniel, E. Valentine. *Charred Lullabies: Chapters in an Anthropology of Violence*. Princeton, N. J.: Princeton University Press, 1996.

Dillistone, F. W., ed. *Myth and Symbol*. London, U. K.: S.P.C.K. 1966.

Dunne, John S. *The City of the Gods: A Study in Myth and Mortality*. Notre Dame, Ind.: Notre Dame Press, 1978.

Eller, Jack David. *From Culture to Ethnicity to Conflict: An Anthropological Perspective on International Ethnic Conflict*. Ann Arbor, Mich.: University of Michigan Press, 1999.

Girard, René. *Violence and the Sacred*. tr. Patrick Gregory. Baltimore: Johns Hopkins University Press, 1979.

Hamerton-Kelly, Robert G., ed. *Violent Origins*. Stanford, Calif.: Stanford University Press, 1987.

Haught, James A. *Holy Hatred: Religious Conflicts of the Nineties*. Amherst, N. Y.: Prometheus Books, 1995.

Henry, William E., and Nevitt Sanford, eds. *Sanctions For Evil*. San Francisco: Jossey-Bass Inc., 1971.

Levinas, Emmanuel. *Totality and Infinity: An Essay on Exteriority*. tr. Alfonso Lingis. Pittsburg: Duquesne University Press, 1969.

———. *Existence and Existents*. tr. Alfonso Lingis. Dordrecht, Netherlands: Kluwer Academic Publishers, 1978.

———. *Otherwise Than Being or Beyond Essence*. tr. Alfonso Lingis. Dordrecht, Netherlands: Kluwer Academic Publishers, 1991.

————. *Collected Philosophical Papers*. tr. Alfonso Lingis. Dordrecht, Netherlands: Kluwer Academic Publishers, 1993.

Lincoln, Bruce. *Death, War and Sacrifice: Studies in Ideologies and Practice*. Chicago: University of Chicago Press, 1991.

Lonsdale, Steven H. *Dance and Ritual Play in Greek Religion*. Baltimore: Johns Hopkins University Press, 1993.

Lorenz, Konrad. *On Aggression*. tr. Marjorie Kerr Wilson. New York: Harcourt, Brace and World, 1966.

Lystad, Mary. *Violence in the Home: Interdisciplinary Perspectives*. Philadelphia: Brunner-Routledge, 1986.

May, Rollo. *Power and Innocence: A Search for the Sources of Violence*. New York: Norton and Co., 1972.

Neusner, Jacob, ed. *Religion and the Political Order*. Atlanta: Scholars' Press, 1996.

Shaughnessey, James D., ed. *The Roots of Ritual*. Grand Rapids, Mich.: B. Eerdman Publishing, 1973.

Sluka, Jeffrey A., ed. *Death Squad: An Anthropology of State Terror*. Philadelphia: University of Pennsylvania Press, 2000.

Smith, Christian, ed. *Disruptive Religion: The Force of Faith in Social-Movement Activism*. New York: Routledge, 1996.

Stivers, Richard. *Evil in Modern Myth and Ritual*. Athens, Georgia: University of Georgia Press, 1991.

Index

About the Author

Wendy C. Hamblet is a Canadian philosopher who holds a Masters Degree in Philosophy from Brock University in Canada and an M.A./ Ph.D. in Philosophy from The Pennsylvania State University. Professor Hamblet is currently teaching Philosophy (Moral Issues, Ancient Philosophy, Ethics and Politics) at Adelphi University, New York. Her research focuses upon the problems of peaceful engagement within and among human communities, especially for communities that have suffered histories of radical victimization. Her papers are widely published in professional journals, including *The Monist, Prima Philosophia, Existentia, Philosophical Writings*, and *Ethica*. Professor Hamblet is an alumnus of the *Center for Advanced Holocaust Studies* at the United States Holocaust Memorial Museum in Washington D.C. and she is affiliated with the *International Association of Genocide Scholars* and *Concerned Philosophers For Peace* (as co-director of the Pacific Division of CPP and Associate Editor of the CPP *Newsletter*).